SOUTH AFRICAN
FACT BOOK

THE
SOUTH AFRICAN
FACT BOOK

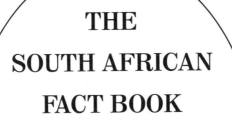

**Jabulile Bongiwe Ngwenya,
Denise Slabbert
and Pat Hopkins**

PENGUIN BOOKS

PENGUIN BOOKS

Published by the Penguin Group
Penguin Books (South Africa) (Pty) Ltd, 24 Sturdee Avenue, Rosebank, Johannesburg 2196, South Africa
Penguin Books Ltd, 80 Strand, London WC2R 0RL, England
Penguin Group (USA) Inc, 375 Hudson Street, New York, New York 10014, USA
Penguin Group (Canada), 90 Eglinton Avenue East, Suite 700, Toronto, Ontario, M4P 2Y3, Canada (a division of Pearson Penguin Canada Inc.)
Penguin Ireland, 25 St Stephen's Green, Dublin 2, Ireland (a division of Penguin Books Ltd)
Penguin Group (Australia), 250 Camberwell Road, Camberwell, Victoria 3124, Australia (a division of Pearson Australia Group Pty Ltd)
Penguin Books India Pvt Ltd, 11 Community Centre, Panchsheel Park, New Delhi – 110 017, India
Penguin Group (NZ), 67 Apollo Drive, Mairangi Bay, Auckland 1310, New Zealand (a division of Pearson New Zealand Ltd)

Penguin Books (South Africa) (Pty) Ltd, Registered Offices:
24 Sturdee Avenue, Rosebank, Johannesburg 2196, South Africa

www.penguinbooks.co.za

First published by Penguin Books (South Africa) (Pty) Ltd 2009
Reprinted 2010

Copyright © Jabulile Bongiwe Ngwenya, Denise Slabbert and Pat Hopkins 2009

ISBN 9780143026051

Typeset by Nix design in 11/14 pt Elegant Garamond
Cover design: luckyfish
Printed and bound by Interpak Books, Pietermaritzburg

CONTENTS

Foreword

The South African story
(and we're sticking to it)

Historic timeline   5

Useless information

Location   45

Area   45

Landform   45

Climate   45

Government   46

Provinces and capitals   47

National symbols   47

National anthem   48

Public holidays   51

Population   52

Cultural villages   62

Religion   63

Economy   67

Health   70

Communications   72

Transportation   72

Crime and occasional punishment   76

Historic attractions

Museums and monuments   81

Battlefields and heritage sites   101

Natural attractions

World Heritage Sites   111

UNESCO Biosphere Reserves   117

South African biomes   119

Transfrontier, National and Ezemvelo KZN Parks   123

Mammals   133

Ramsar sites   136

Botanical gardens   139

Blue Flag beaches   140

Outdoor activities and adventures   142

Urban distractions

City vibe   149

Small towns   150

Zoos   158

Culture

Arts and crafts   161

Music   163

Dance   166

Radio, film and television   166

Theatre   169

Literature   172

Food and drink   173

Sport   186

Index   196

FOREWORD

In the global scheme of things South Africa should really be an insignificant backwater, but is known to punch above its weight. It is the proverbial little guy with big balls, like minute boxer Baby Jake Matlala, who in 2002 became the first South African to win four world titles when he defeated Colombian Juan Herrera for the WBU junior flyweight championship. Why is this? Well, the facts speak for themselves.

We maintain it is because of a genetic abnormality leeched into the soil tens of thousands of years ago when the first humans emerged here. They were way down the food chain, but adapted to take on all comers, move on to populate the world and then become the most dominant species of all time. As people of all hues came back to South Africa, they were possessed with a trait that everything is possible. That is why we have some of the most recognisable political icons on earth, young people who believe they can go into space (and do), drivers who are convinced they are immortal no matter the risks they take and gangsters who think they can get away with anything.

The facts tell us that this is a mad, fascinating, bad, mystical country. They also tell us that it is a compelling, colourful place in a world increasingly defined by anaemia. Because of this no book can present every fact that makes South Africa the greatest place on earth. But hopefully we will give you enough to take pride in our home, cringe at some of our family members, laugh a bit, then resolve to add a few facts of your own before you depart either this life or our shores. Whatever your contribution, it will enrich our character even more and we will be eternally grateful.

This book will attempt to tell the story of South Africa through a selection of facts. We will also in places give what might appear to be an opinion, but these are our incontrovertible facts on what to do or avoid, depending on your interest. If we have missed any glaringly obvious facts that you would like to bring to our attention, or if you feel deeply offended by our tongue-in-cheek 'facts', then our basic instinct as blue-blooded South Africans would be to tell you to take a hike in somewhat more colourful language. But our publisher has its happy feet in other climes and insists we be more civil and invite you rather to log your contribution/rant. Go to the Penguin Books South Africa website (www.penguinbooks.co.za) for more details.

The

SOUTH AFRICAN
Story

(and we're sticking to it)

South Africa is an ancient land. Here you can see evidence of the formation of our planet, walk in the footsteps of dinosaurs and trace your roots back to the first people.

As the earth cooled during the Archaean period 3,2 billion years ago, so the first rocks were formed. Amongst the oldest are along the Greenstone Belt, stretching from northern KwaZulu-Natal to the Soutpansberg Mountains in Limpopo Province, with the best examples near Barberton in Mpumalanga. A billion or so years later a massive meteorite slammed into what is now the Vredefort Dome, a World Heritage Site near the Free State town of Parys.

That was not the end of our cataclysmic formation. Much of the country lay under an inland sea on the super-continent of Gondwana until its plates first collided then tore apart to form Africa, South America, Australia, the Indian subcontinent and Antarctica some 400 million years ago. The effects of this can still be seen along the serrated, mountainous coastline of the Western Cape.

It would be another 200 million years before dinosaurs appeared, leaving magnificent fossil records in the Beaufort Group of rocks of the Karoo. They disappeared in one of the great extinctions, opening the way for the ascendancy of Man. More than 3 million years ago pre-human australopithecines or southern apemen roamed southern Africa. Now the search for the roots of human existence is focused on the cave system beneath the Sterkfontein Valley, which is part of the Cradle of Humankind World Heritage Site near Johannesburg.

These apemen would evolve into the earliest humans, who scoured the coastline for shellfish from Langebaan in the Western Cape to Border Cave in KwaZulu-Natal, and kept on going to populate the world – leaving behind the Bushmen (San), whose rock art is our earliest historical record.

It is the return of their descendants in a great diversity of races and cultures that shaped modern South Africa. The Khoi came back two millennia ago, followed by advancing Iron Age black groups moving south from the northern and eastern regions of the continent.

By AD 1100 Mapungubwe in the Limpopo Valley was the seat of the greatest kingdom in southern Africa. Now a major historical attraction and national park, it traded gold and ivory with the Middle and Far East. In 1488 the Portuguese mariner Bartholomeu Dias rounded the Cape and discovered the south-eastern entry to the Indian Ocean, heralding an astonishing period of European empire building. This led to the Dutch establishing a refreshment station in 1652 in what is now Cape Town.

International politics and the discovery of the country's massive mineral wealth brought other settlers from around the globe. What ensued was a bloody quest for domination and survival that would ultimately shape the borders of the country. It was a conflict that coalesced into a racial war and the heroic Struggle for Freedom, which culminated in liberation from oppression in 1994.

3,2 billion years ago

As the earth cooled during the Archaean period, so the first rocks were formed. Amongst the oldest rocks on earth are those along the Greenstone Belt stretching from northern KwaZulu-Natal to the Soutpansberg Mountains in Limpopo.

2 billion years ago

A massive meteorite slammed into earth near the present Free State town of Parys, now a World Heritage Site known as the Vredefort Dome.

400 million years ago

Much of South Africa lay under an inland sea on the super-continent of Gondwana.

200 million years ago

The first dinosaurs appeared.

More than 3 million years ago

Pre-human australopithecines or southern apemen roamed southern Africa.

2 million years ago

Our earliest ancestors were the first to intentionally occupy a cave and use stone tools at Wonderwerk Cave (Miracle Cave) near Kuruman in the Northern

Cape. This is just the latest in a string of discoveries in this massive grotto that has revealed so much about human evolution and environmental change.

117 000 years ago

Evidence has been found of some of the earliest human existence at Border Cave in KwaZulu-Natal and Tsitsikamma and Langebaan in the Western Cape.

2 000 years ago

The Khoi entered South Africa, bringing with them domestic animals. These pastoralists settled mainly in the fertile valleys of the southern Cape coast, but were later forced into drier areas by advancing black groups moving south from the northern and eastern regions of Africa. These Africans brought the Iron Age to southern Africa. Today the Khoi and remaining Bushmen make up the Khoisan culture.

900 years ago

Mapungubwe in the Limpopo Valley was the seat of the greatest kingdom in southern Africa. It traded gold and ivory with the Middle and Far East. For reasons unknown it was abandoned after 400 years, with the inhabitants moving north to found Great Zimbabwe and south to places like Thulamela. Those going north became the Shona-speaking people, and those migrating south, the Venda.

January 1488

Bartholomeu Dias rounded the Cape and discovered the south-eastern entry to the Indian Ocean – heralding an astonishing period of European empire building. He got as far as Algoa Bay before mutiny forced him to return to Portugal.

5 April 1652

Jan van Riebeeck arrived in Table Bay and established a refreshment station for merchantmen of the Dutch East India Company. Seafarers had been awestruck by the magnificence of the mountains of the Cape Peninsula. Amidst it all is the iconic Table Mountain, which rises from Table Bay and can be seen from 200 kilometres out to sea. For nearly two centuries Table Bay was used as a refreshment and repair stop by passing European ships.

1657

The Dutch East India Company sent the first slaves to Cape Town. These came mainly from East Africa and South-East Asia, as the Company had forbidden Van Riebeeck from enslaving the local population.

2 January 1666

Work commenced on the Castle of Good Hope. Designed by the famous Dutch architect Menno van Coehoorn, it was completed in 1679. It is designed in the shape of a pentagon with bastions dedicated to the titles of the Prince of Orange at each point.

Did you know?

> The Castle of Good Hope is the oldest building still in use in South Africa.

1685

The first French Huguenots arrived after fleeing religious persecution in their homeland. They were largely responsible for establishing the wine industry of the Western Cape and together with the Dutch became the forefathers of the Afrikaner people.

1743

A seasonal outstation was established in False Bay at what was to become Simon's Town. Before long there was a fort and a smattering of buildings, but in those early years it was fairly dour for a port. The character of the town changed completely when the British decided in 1814 to convert it into a naval base for the South Atlantic Squadron, then in a desperate battle against slavers. Today it is the headquarters of the South African Navy.

1785

Shaka was born. His father was a minor chief and his mother unranked, but he still went on to mould the Zulu nation through conquering the Nguni clans of present-day KwaZulu-Natal. While he was a great military strategist, his reign was largely responsible for the *Mfecane* (forced dispersal) of the early 1800s, in which people fled his forces. These in turn either conquered groups to the north and in the interior, or were absorbed by more powerful communities. This strife left large areas of the interior unpopulated at a time when restive Boers were looking north from the Cape Colony. Shaka was assassinated by a group led by his half-brother Dingane in 1828.

1795

The first British occupation of the Cape began, with little resistance from the Dutch East India Company. It was handed back to the Dutch in 1803, but forcibly reoccupied two years later. It was formally ceded to Britain in 1814, with Lord Charles Somerset as governor.

August 1799

Port Elizabeth, 'The Friendly City', was founded. The need for a port in the Eastern Cape became more pressing with each eastward push of the Cape frontier. First named Fort Frederick, it was renamed Port Elizabeth in the early 1820s. Today this elegant city is home to motor manufacturers and attracts visitors to its beautiful beaches.

1812

Grahamstown was founded. The Great Fish River in the early nineteenth century was the turbulent eastern frontier of the Cape Colony that had recently been acquired by the British. Today Grahamstown is filled with the romanticism of a bygone era. It is steeped in history, legend and mystique that veil it like the mists that roll in from the nearby ocean. It is renowned for hosting one of the great art festivals, the Grahamstown Arts Festival, over eleven days each June/July.

April 1820

The 1820 Settlers arrived. The mystic Makana and 10 000 followers had attacked Grahamstown on 22 April 1819. Somerset had called for Britain to send emigrants to bolster the defences of the colony, and these appeals now became more urgent. Britain, in the grip of depression since the end of the Napoleonic wars in 1815, seized the opportunity to rid itself of some of its excess population. Farms and transport were offered for nearly 4 000 men, women and children through extravagant advertisements that gave no warning of the risks involved. After arriving, most were forced to move to Grahamstown, unable to survive in an alien, hostile environment plagued by droughts and floods.

1823

Lieutenants James King and George Farewell on a trading expedition to St Lucia Bay found refuge from bad weather in a bay to the south, which until then was thought to be blocked by a sand bar. Basing themselves on Salisbury Island at the entrance, they charted what was to become Port Natal. The following year Farewell organised a party under Henry Francis Fynn, who obtained a grant of land around the bay from then Zulu king Shaka and there established a trading and ivory-hunting post. Among the first to settle here were Alexander Biggar and a very young Richard (Dick) King, who would go on to become 'the saviour of Natal'. The town grew and in June 1835 the residents decided to change its name to D'Urban (subsequently Durban), in honour of Cape Governor Sir Benjamin D'Urban.

Did you know?

While Shaka's successor, Dingane, clashed on numerous occasions with Henry Fynn, Fynn was nevertheless recognised as a 'great chief' in 1831 and given nine wives – three of which he passed on to his brother Frank.

1834

Slavery was abolished throughout the British Empire. This proved highly unpopular with the Boers of the Cape, becoming the focal issue for greater disaffection with British rule.

Late 1835

About 15 000 Boers began a mass exodus of the Cape Colony in what has come to be known as the Great Trek. The migration of a significant number of well-armed people with specific ideas about racial superiority into an interior already in turmoil was to have a massive impact on southern African history. Beyond the border they fanned out, with most choosing to continue either into the central interior or north-east over the Drakensberg into present-day

KwaZulu-Natal with its safe harbour that promised access to a sympathetic outside world.

16 December 1838

The most significant of the Boer groups that chose the east coast were headed by Gerrit Maritz and Piet Retief, who had arrived in late 1837, and those under Piet Uys and Andries Pretorius followed shortly afterwards. Zulu king Dingane took fright at the arrival of large numbers of settlers, which led to the massacre of Retief and the ambushing of Uys before the Zulus were defeated at Blood River on 16 December 1838. After this the trekkers declared the short-lived Republic of Natalia (later to become Natal) with Pretorius as president and Pietermaritzburg in the Umzunduze Valley as capital.

1842

The Cape governor Sir George Napier ordered Captain Thomas Charlton Smith, a veteran of Waterloo, to march with a company of 263 men from the fortified post at Umazi River near Port St Johns to Durban. Smith, on arrival, tore down the Boer flag at Fort Victoria. But he did not occupy it, choosing to build a new one at his camp, which is now the Old Fort. Smith attacked the Boer position at Congella on the night of 23 May 1842, but his force was repulsed and, with six-pounder guns captured from the British, the Boers laid siege to him in the Old Fort.

Did you know?

Dick King, who was on board the trading vessel *Mazeppa* when the Battle of Congella took place, was approached on 25 May by Durban trader GC Cato to take a message from Captain Thomas Charlton Smith to the garrison at Fort Pedi near Grahamstown. To avoid Boer lookouts, he was ferried with his 16-year-old servant, Ndongeni, and two horses to Salisbury Island, from where they followed a secret path back to the mainland. Riding 1 000 kilometres over rough, dangerous countryside during which they crossed 122 rivers, King reached Grahamstown 10 days later. Reinforcements were dispatched by sea via Port Elizabeth, and they arrived in Durban between 24 and 26 June to lift the siege.

1845

The British annexed Natal as a dependency of the Cape, which led to most of the Boers in that territory again trekking into the interior. There they predominantly settled the areas that were to become the Boer republics of the Orange Free State and Zuid-Afrikaansche Republiek (Transvaal Republic). Natal was separated from the Cape and given its own administration in 1856.

1854

The Boer leader Commandant-General Marthinus Wessels Pretorius, son of the hero of Blood River, Andries Pretorius, purchased land at Elandspoort for a church square to serve the central Boer Zuid-Afrikaansche Republiek. Within a year a town had developed round the church square and it was christened Pretoria Philadelphia – in honour of the Pretorius family and the brotherhood of Voortrekkers but later shortened to Pretoria, which succeeded Potchefstroom as capital of the new state.

April 1856

Based on a redemptive vision by a teenage girl from the Centane district, Nongqawuse, the Xhosa slaughtered their cattle and destroyed their crops. This act devastated them, leading to mass starvation and impoverishment. It so weakened the nation that it eased white incursions into their area.

1877

Britain annexed the Boer republic called the Transvaal, which led to the start of the first Anglo-Boer War (known by the Boers as the War of Independence) in 1880. After a humiliating defeat at Majuba Hill, the British restored sovereignty to the republic.

1879

British forces invaded Zululand in order to subjugate the Zulu people under Cetshwayo. While the Zulu won battles at Isandlwana, Hlobane and Intombi Spruit, they were eventually defeated by superior firepower. This was followed by imperial campaigns against the

Bapedi and Basotho. Zululand was annexed in 1887 and a decade later incorporated into Natal.

9 May 1883

Paul Kruger became president of the Transvaal. Born in the Eastern Cape, he had trekked into the interior as a boy with his family.

1890

Cecil John Rhodes became prime minister of the Cape Colony.

1893

Natal was granted self-government. Soon after Mohandas (Mahatma) Gandhi arrived there to practise law. He was met by local businessman Abdulla Seth, who had arranged for him to travel by train to Pretoria a week later to observe a trial. He only intended to spend one year in South Africa, but his experiences on that journey were so formative that he stayed for 20 – a time in which he conceived his programme of enlightened passive resistance. In 1913 he returned to India where he emerged in 1920 as leader for that country's independence.

Did you know?

Mahatma Gandhi was the first lawyer of colour to be admitted to the Supreme Court in South Africa.

30 December 1896

Leander Starr Jameson led a force into the Transvaal, ostensibly to liberate the citizens of Johannesburg but in reality to gain control of the Witwatersrand goldfields for Britain. This thinly disguised coup attempt, known as the Jameson Raid, was a fiasco and the leaders were captured and tried. But the effects were calamitous as it contributed directly to the second Anglo-Boer War and heightened tensions between Britain and Germany, which culminated in World War I. It also led to the resignation of Cecil John Rhodes as prime minister of the Cape Colony on 5 January 1897.

1899

Enoch Sontonga composed *Nkosi Sikelel' iAfrika* (God Bless Africa) for the ordination of the first black Methodist minister at Nancefield in Johannesburg. Though it only appeared in print in 1927, it would go on to become the anthem for Zambia and the South African liberation movement.

11 October 1899

The Anglo-Boer War started after the expiry of an ultimatum from Transvaal president Paul Kruger demanding the withdrawal of British troops from the republic's borders. The Orange Free State was automatically drawn into the conflict through treaties with the Transvaal. Hostilities began that evening when Boers led by General Koos de la Rey ambushed a train at Kraaipan.

Did you know?

The first shot of the Boer War was fired by Boer gunner Jaap van Deventer who, ironically, was knighted after the war for services to the British Empire.

5 June 1900

The conventional phase of the Anglo-Boer War ended when Field-Marshall Lord Roberts entered Pretoria and tore down the *Vierkleur*, the Transvaal flag. Shortly before, President Kruger had left by rail for Portuguese East Africa and on to exile in Switzerland. It appeared that hostilities would soon be over, but in reality this was the opening scene for the brutal guerrilla war that followed.

8 September 1901

Future prime minister and architect of apartheid, Dr Hendrik Frensch Verwoerd, was born in Amsterdam and arrived in southern Africa with his parents two years later. In the 1920s he studied at three German universities and there came into contact with fanatical Nazi ideology, ideas he brought back with him to Stellenbosch in the Western Cape in 1928.

31 May 1902

The Anglo-Boer War ended with the signing of the Peace of Vereeniging. The document avoided the term 'surrender' and accorded colonial status on the defeated republics. While the Great Trek and the war left deep scars and formed the core of future introspective nationalist philosophy and mythology, they might never have found currency but for High Commissioner Lord Alfred Milner's aggressive post-war Anglicisation policy.

September 1903

Afrikaners, frustrated at being refused permission to teach their children in their mother tongue, began establishing private Afrikaans schools – the forerunners to Christian National Education in the latter part of the twentieth century.

1904

When gold-mining resumed after the British occupation of Johannesburg in 1900, there was a rapid influx of blacks. They crammed into the inner-city slums that one report described as unsanitary 'dark dens'. But it was not the health risks so much as different groups 'living on friendly terms' that concerned the authorities. An outbreak of bubonic plague in 1904 gave them the excuse to remove 1 358 black residents 13 kilometres from Johannesburg to what would become Soweto.

1905

The political direction South Africa was taking was becoming clear. The British imperial government, to reconcile with the ex-Boer republics, was anxious these colonies be granted responsible self-goverment as soon as possible. This meant segregation to maintain white economic and political domination, and a key element of this thinking was that black and white land be separated.

Led by Chief Bambatha, thousands mainly of Zulus rose in rebellion against a poll tax on all unmarried men. Bambatha was killed during the final battle at Nkandla.

12 October 1908

The South African National Convention was constituted with the mandate of uniting the Cape Colony, Orange Free State, Transvaal and Natal into one nation. It completed its deliberations on 11 May 1909, and among its recommendations were that Cape Town be the seat of Parliament and the legislative capital, Pretoria the administrative capital and Bloemfontein the judicial capital. Today South Africa still has three capitals. It also drew a draft constitution, in which English and Dutch were accorded equal status.

24-6 March 1909

The South African Native Convention was held in Bloemfontein. It was the first national gathering of black representatives, who met so they could present a united front to the grave danger inherent in the proposed union, but this had little impact on the imperial government.

31 May 1910

The Union of South Africa came into being. General Louis Botha won the first general election, in which only white males could vote, on 15 September 1910 and was asked to form a government.

1911

The South African National Party (later the South African Party then the United Party) was formed.

8 January 1912

The forerunner to the African National Congress was founded. As the realisation dawned that the new Union of South Africa only meant worse was to come, blacks began discussing in 1911 the formation of a new organisation to represent them. Envisaged was a movement that would unite politically active black organisations, bring in the chiefs as representatives of traditional society and promote the aspirations of emerging black leaders. Later that year it was finally agreed to hold an inaugural conference. Pixley Seme, an attorney, opened the convention and concluded with a proposal that a permanent congress be established. The motion was unanimously accepted and the Reverend John Dube was elected president and Sol Plaatje the first Secretary-General of what was christened the South African Native National Congress (SANNC) – to be changed a few years later to the African National Congress (ANC).

1912

South Africa got its own defence force, commanded by General Beyers, when the South African Defence Force Act was passed.

1913

The National Party was founded after a split in the South African National Party.

June 1913

The Natives Land Act was passed, which laid the foundation for apartheid and the mass suppression of blacks. This cynical piece of legislation, in which Britain acquiesced, was drafted to satisfy white aspirations for segregation while satisfying the labour needs of predominantly Afrikaner farmers and English mine and business owners by depriving blacks of the right to acquire land outside limited demarcated areas.

9 September 1914

South Africa declared war on Germany and entered World War I. The decision was not popular among certain sections of the Afrikaner community who sympathised with Germany, and a rebellion flared that was only suppressed early the following year. After this, South Africa occupied German South West Africa (today Namibia) in 1915 and led the campaign to take German East Africa. In Europe, South Africans acquitted themselves on the Western Front, in particular suffering heavy losses in the battle of Delville Wood near the French village of Longueval. In the final stages of the war, an influenza epidemic killed millions worldwide, including nearly 140 000 South Africans.

17 April 1918

A National Party meeting in Johannesburg, addressed by Cape leader Dr DF Malan, was broken up in a free-for-all in which party members were assaulted. The following day three teenage Afrikaners who attended the meeting, Henning Klopper, Danie du Plessis and HW van der Merwe, vowed to form an organisation that would fulfil Afrikaner dreams. On 5 June the group met again and formed a secret society called Jong Suid Afrika (Young South Africa) – later to become the Afrikaner Broederbond (Brotherhood), which was instrumental in the National Party victory in the 1948 general election.

18 July 1918

Nelson Rolihlahla Mandela was born in the Eastern Cape.

1921

The Communist Party of South Africa was formed.

28 February 1922

The Rand Revolt began on the Witwatersrand when police shot dead three white miners taking part in a strike over wage and workforce cuts and the opening of semi-skilled jobs for blacks. The rebels held large parts of Johannesburg before order was restored by martial law on 14 March. Nearly 700 were killed or injured in the uprising and the anger of workers led directly to Prime Minister Jan Smuts being swept from office to be replaced by the National Party, which settled the issue of the opening of semi-skilled jobs for blacks by introducing a formal 'colour bar' in mining and industry to protect white workers. From now on the development of black skills was to be subordinated to the needs of white labour.

1924

The fossilised skull known as the Taung Child was found in the limestone quarries at Buxton near Taung in the

North West province by Professor Raymond Dart.
His search for an adult specimen led to the discovery
in 1947 of an adult *Australopithecus africanus*, dubbed
Mrs Ples, in the caves at Sterkfontein and Kromdraai.
This area is now the Cradle of Humankind World
Heritage Site.

1925

Afrikaans, a South African language with origins in
Dutch, Malay, Portuguese, French, German and indigenous Khoi and African languages, replaced Dutch as
an official language.

31 May 1928

A South African flag was flown for the first time
alongside the Union Jack. It comprised the orange,
white and blue of the Dutch *Prinsenvlag* and incorporated a central design of the old South African
Republic and Orange Free State flags with the Union
Jack.

14 May 1930

White women received the vote when the Women's
Enfranchisement Bill was passed. It was known as
Bertha's Bill, in recognition of the efforts of Advocate
Bertha Solomons to achieve gender equality.

1933

The South African Party and National Party formed
a coalition known as the United Party. Dr DF Malan
refused to join and formed the Purified National
Party, later to become the National Party.

8 August 1938

The *Eufees Trek* (Centenary Trek) got underway in Cape Town bound for Monument Koppie in Pretoria, where the foundation stone of the Voortrekker Monument was to be laid. Organised by the Broederbond, it was a masterstroke in that it helped unite Afrikaners – contributing directly to the National Party election victory a decade later, which ushered in apartheid. It is also credited with turning the *braaivleis* (barbeque) into a national culinary tradition.

22 December 1938

Marjorie Courtenay-Latimer, the curator of the East London Museum, was presented with a fish by local fishermen. It was later identified by Professor JLB Smith of Rhodes University as a coelacanth (dubbed *Old Fourlegs* because of its unique protuberances), thought to have been extinct for 70 million years – then predating anything in recorded history.

4 September 1939

A day after Britain declared war on Nazi Germany, the South African parliament voted in favour of participation. This was a divisive issue, with Prime Minister General Albert Hertzog favouring neutrality. But opposition leader General Jan Smuts prevailed and was asked to form a new government. Local forces played a major part in the Desert War and Italian Campaign.

December 1943

The ANC Youth League was founded. An Africanist

faction within the movement was becoming increasingly discontented at the inability of the party to
mobilise the masses, an incapacity they feared
would marginalise the movement. Included in this
group were young activists Walter Sisulu, Peter Mda,
Anton Lembede, Oliver Tambo and the 25-year-old
Mandela, who together formed the Congress Youth
League – with Lembede as president and Mandela as
an executive member. Its formation was approved at
the ANC annual congress in Bloemfontein.

17 February 1947

The first visit to South Africa by a reigning British
monarch started when HMS *Vanguard* docked at
Cape Town. The royal party included King George VI,
Queen Elizabeth and their two daughters. Princess
Elizabeth, soon to succeed her father, celebrated
her 21st birthday in Cape Town before touring the
country.

26 May 1948

DF Malan's National Party triumphed at the polls,
which allowed their fanciful brand of National
Socialism to be given effect. There were many reasons
for their surprise victory: they offered a package of
promises that appealed to white workers, farmers,
professionals and intellectuals; they benefited from
the weighting of the rural vote; they exploited white
fears attendant on mass black urbanisation while
the governing United Party led by an elderly Smuts
seemed increasingly out of touch with local sentiment.
But, more than anything else, they offered apartheid
in simple, easy-to-grasp terms.

1948

The South African Bureau for Racial Affairs (SABRA) was launched to give effect to the philosophy of apartheid. Their 'scientific study' led directly to the Prohibition of Mixed Marriages Act, introduced in 1949, which outlawed marriages between white and non-white; the Immorality Act which made sexual relations across the colour line illegal; the Population Registration Act of 1950 which assigned every person in the borders of South Africa to one of four broad racial categories (white, black, coloured and Asian) and governed how each would be organised and administered; and, the 'very essence of apartheid', the Group Areas Act, which enforced separate urban areas for each race group.

1950

Race riots in Johannesburg as blacks mounted opposition to race policies.

1954

DF Malan was succeeded as prime minister by JG Strijdom.

9 February 1955

Under apartheid, efforts were intensified to clear Johannesburg of blacks and racially mixed suburbs. The most famous of these was the vibrant Sophiatown, the creative soul of the city, established in 1904. At its heart was the Anglican Church of Christ the King, made famous by Archbishop Trevor Huddleston, who ministered there in the 1940s and 50s. It was promulgated that its residents were to be moved from February 1955. Under the slogan 'We won't move', they resisted removal. In this they were supported by Huddleston, Nelson Mandela, Helen Joseph and Ruth First, but on 9 February thousands of heavily armed policemen and troops entered the township. Over the next eight years the 65 000 residents were taken to Meadowlands in Soweto, Lenasia and Westbury.

1955

An all-race Congress of the People organised by the ANC and held at Kliptown in Soweto adopted a charter of demands, the Freedom Charter, on behalf of the disenfranchised black population. It reaffirmed multiracialism.

1956

The Riotous Assemblies Act was passed, as was the Separate Representation of Voters Act, which finally removed coloureds from the common roll.

May 1957

CJ Langenhoven's 1918 song, 'Die Stem' (The Voice), was accepted as the national anthem.

1958

Prime Minister JG Strijdom resigned and was succeeded by Hendrik Verwoerd. In the mid-1950s the Tomlinson Commission – an initiative of Verwoerd's Ministry of Native Affairs – issued its report that would form the basis for the Promotion of Bantu Self-Government Act that created eight ethnic

Bantustans, later called homelands, which became the foundation for grand apartheid. The central premise of the Homeland Policy was that there was no black majority, but rather groups of ethnic minorities of which whites were one. In any case, only the whites were South Africans as all the black splinter groups belonged in clearly defined areas to be excised from South Africa and eventually given independence, making them 'temporary sojourners' in the land of their birth.

17 August 1959

Seven members of Parliament resigned from the opposition United Party to form the Progressive Party. Of these, only Helen Suzman would retain her seat in the next general election in 1961 – remaining the lonely voice of white liberal consciousness until the elections of 1974.

1959

The Pan Africanist Congress (PAC) was founded. Because of the support the ANC received from other sections of the community, many of the Youth League leaders (including Tambo, Mandela and Sisulu) began to have second thoughts about Africanism. This group, as they embraced multiracialism, moved away from the positions still held by die-hard Africanists like Zeph Mothopeng and Robert Sobukwe, who broke away to form the PAC.

21 March 1960

Police opened fire on a peaceful black anti-pass law

(by which the movement of blacks was restricted) demonstration in the Vereeniging township of Sharpeville – leaving 69 dead and 200 injured, many of whom were shot in the back. The brutality of the state's reaction forever changed world opinion on its policies. The Sharpeville Massacre, as it came to be known, led directly to the armed struggle for liberation, the country's growing isolation and the banning of the ANC and PAC on 8 April as part of a state of emergency.

9 April 1960

Prime Minister Verwoerd survived an assassination attempt at the Rand Show when disaffected wealthy farmer David Platt walked up to him and shot him twice in the head.

October 1960

In a referendum, white South Africa voted for republican status.

December 1960

ANC president Chief Albert Luthuli was awarded the Nobel Peace Prize. He was president of the ANC until he was killed in suspicious circumstances by a train in July 1967.

31 May 1961

South Africa became a republic, withdrawing from the Commonwealth a short while later. From then on the country was known as the Republic of South Africa.

16 December 1961

The ANC established a military division, Umkhonto we Sizwe (MK – Spear of the Nation), to destroy government property. Three months previously the PAC had formed its own armed structure, uPoqo (Pure).

1963

Police raided a house in Rivonia, Liliesleaf Farm, which had been used as the headquarters of MK. This led to the charging under the General Law Amendment Act (Sabotage Act) and the Suppression of Communism Act of nine people in what became known as the Rivonia Treason Trial. On 12 June the following year Judge Quartus de Wet sentenced eight of the accused to life imprisonment – including Nelson Mandela, Ahmed Kathrada and Govan Mbeki (the father of former president Thabo Mbeki). Soon after, the trialists were transported to Robben Island, where Mandela was incarcerated for most of the 27 years he spent behind bars.

1963

The Transkei was given self-governing status as part of the grand apartheid homeland system. This was extended to full 'independence' in 1976. Bophutha-tswana, Ciskei and Venda followed in the late 1970s. Most blacks were bitterly opposed to this system.

24 July 1964

Schoolteacher Frederick John Harris of the short-lived African Resistance Movement (ARM) hid a time bomb

at Johannesburg Station, which killed one person and
injured 22. On 1 April 1965 he was hanged at Pretoria
Central Prison.

6 September 1966

Prime Minister Verwoerd, having taken his seat
in the House of Assembly to address Parliament,
was stabbed to death by parliamentary messenger
Dimitrio Tsafendas. Tsafendas was committed to an
asylum until shortly before his death.

1966

Verwoerd was succeeded by BJ Vorster, who was
interned during World War II as a member of the Nazi-
sympathising Ossewabrandwag. From this position
as Minister of Justice he built the security apparatus
that transformed South Africa into a notoriously
repressive police state.

1966

District Six, the sixth municipal district in Cape
Town, was established in 1867 as a racially mixed
community of freed slaves, merchants, artisans,
labourers and immigrants. With close links to the city
and port, it was renowned for its vibrancy. First to
be forcibly removed were blacks in 1901. In 1966 it
was declared a white area and over the next decade
and a half, 60 000 coloured residents were relocated
to faceless townships on the Cape Flats, their houses
flattened by bulldozers.

1967

> Oliver Tambo became president of the ANC after the death of Albert Luthuli.

1969

> Steve Biko and Barney Pityana founded the South African Students' Organisation, which promoted the ideology of Black Consciousness (BC). While the roots of BC lay in white liberalism, it was defined by the American Black Power Movement. Its philosophy made some inroads into the black adult community – particularly through their Black Community Programme focused on literacy, adult education, health and employment designed to show solidarity with the masses. Their message of being proud to be black struck a chord, but it was also true that most of the older generation found them too radical and still firmly supported the broad-based ANC. Amongst the school-going youth, however, most identified with its ethos.

1974

> A coup in Portugal led to the revolutionary Samora Machel, leader of the Frelimo liberation movement, taking power in Mozambique in 1975. In Angola competing groups struggled for ascendancy. South Africa's Minister of Defence PW Botha, in a disastrous move in August 1975, clandestinely committed the South African army to support the Angolan UNITA movement of Jonas Savimbi. He had been promised assistance by the CIA, but this was not forthcoming and the MPLA prevailed, supported by Cuban forces and superior Soviet weaponry. South Africa was

forced into a humiliating withdrawal. The upshot was that all its traditional defences altered, leaving it suddenly facing serious security threats over a wide front.

16 June 1976

Police opened fire on protesting students in Soweto, killing student leader Hastings Ndlovu and schoolboy Hector Peterson. This was the culmination of a decision by the government in 1974 to convert Broederbond thought into policy and enforce a 1955 ruling – though not implemented because of a lack of funds – making it compulsory for black schools to teach half the subjects after Grade 3 in Afrikaans and the other half in English. Until then black children were taught for the first three years of school in their mother tongue and beyond that in one of the official languages – English or Afrikaans – selected by the relevant ethnic school board. This became the focal issue for wider anger over discrimination among Black Consciousness-supporting youth, and on 13 June it was decided to stage a march to protest the Afrikaans ruling. Chaos erupted after the shooting, and as news spread so did the uprising. The importance of this event can be measured by the fact that it marked the beginning of the final battle for freedom.

12 September 1977

Steve Biko, who had been detained in August, died of severe injuries from police beatings. He was being transported naked and shackled in the back of a police vehicle from Port Elizabeth to a hospital in Pretoria.

The government banned 17 anti-apartheid organisations and three black newspapers, *The World*, *Weekend World* and *The Voice*.

1978

The biggest political scandal in South African history, the Info Scandal, broke with a fairly lightweight abuse-of-funds story by Kitt Katzin in the *Sunday Express* titled 'Dr Rhoodie's Remarkable Jaunt'. By the time it ran its course it had opened a can of worms about large-scale corruption, fraud and assorted shenanigans, which led to the resignation of Prime Minister Vorster and the fall from grace of National Party heir apparent and Minister of Information, Dr Connie Mulder.

1978

The Info Scandal opened the way for PW Botha to succeed as prime minister. He was armed with the conviction that South Africa was the target of a 'total onslaught' directed from Moscow. This threat was to be met by a 'total strategy' that supplanted Verwoerdian ideology with a security doctrine that had survival as its central theme. To succeed required that apartheid be reformulated to serve the needs of the security-military laager being drawn round every facet of South African life.

24 November 1981

'Mad Mike' Hoare and a group of mercenaries, with clandestine government support, took off from Johannesburg for the Seychelles. Their intention was to topple the Marxist government of Albert René and reinstate James Mancham, who had been ousted in a coup in 1977. For the apartheid state this was an extension of the 'total onslaught' strategy, especially as René had cancelled SAA refuelling rights – further isolating the country. The mission was a debacle from the moment they landed in Mahé, and after a brief gun battle at the airport most of the invaders made it back to South Africa in a hijacked Air India jet, where they were promptly arrested. Ironically, isolation intensified when state involvement in the fiasco was exposed.

20 March 1983

As people left work, a car bomb was detonated in Pretoria's Church Street. Targeting air force head-quarters in the Nedbank Square building, it killed 21, including bombers Freddy Butana Shongwe and Bakayi Ezekiel Maseko, and injured scores. On 23 March the ANC claimed responsibility, which was immediately followed by retaliatory raids on five of the organisation's bases in Maputo.

November 1983

In a referendum, whites voted overwhelmingly for a new constitution, which offered coloureds and Indians a subordinate role in a complex, racially segregated tricameral parliament. For their part, urban blacks were to be given a token share of the political system through Black Local Authorities that would have control over 'own affairs' in townships. Instead of delivering security, the referendum triggered the most serious black revolt in South African history.

Archbishop Desmond Tutu won the Nobel Peace Prize for his opposition to apartheid.

20 July 1985

A state of emergency was imposed to try and deal with increasing unrest among the black population. Though occasionally lifted, it remained largely in place for the rest of the turbulent 80s. Included in its provisions were restrictions on the media.

February 1986

Frederick van Zyl Slabbert breathed fire into moribund white politics when he resigned as leader of the official opposition Progressive Federal Party (PFP) and walked out of Parliament, saying the country was being torn apart and Parliament's reaction was irrelevant. With Dr Alex Boraine he formed the Institute for a Democratic Alternative for South Africa (Idasa), an organisation to build bridges between black and white in anticipation of a democratic South Africa. A year later he sent establishment temperatures soaring when he led a group of Afrikaner opinion makers to West Africa for a week-long meeting, known as the 'Dakar Safari', with the ANC leadership.

February 1989

President Botha's grip on power weakened when he suffered a stroke. While retaining the presidency, he relinquished leadership of the National Party to FW de Klerk, which led to a full-blooded power struggle. Resisting all efforts from within his own party to convince him to stand down, Botha set the scene for a bitter election war when he announced at the beginning of April that Parliament would be dissolved at the end of May with polls in September.

6 September 1989

President FW de Klerk won the general election fought on the need for a negotiated settlement among all sectors of the population as the only path to lasting peace.

2 February 1990

President De Klerk unbanned the ANC, PAC and scores of outlawed organisations.

11 February 1990

Nelson Mandela was released from Victor Verster Prison in Paarl. It was a moment of massive symbolic importance as he had come to symbolise the Struggle for Freedom. De Klerk claimed he had freed Mandela because he was convinced Mandela was committed to peace. But he was forced to, because his choices had narrowed to either negotiation or destruction. South Africa was totally isolated, the pariah of the world, and its state machinery could no longer cope with the boycotts, strikes, stayaways and incursions by freedom fighters.

1991

The Convention for a Democratic South Africa (Codesa) was established to provide a forum to negotiate a transition to democracy. Due to continuing violence, it was dissolved the following year.

But in August 1992 the government and ANC signed a Record of Understanding, which restarted deliberations.

10 April 1993

Secretary-General of the South African Communist Party and Chief of Staff of MK, Martin Thembisele, known as Chris Hani, was assassinated in his driveway by Polish immigrant Janus Walus and Conservative Party member Clive Derby-Lewis. Hani played a key role in the Kempton Park negotiations, which led to agreements on an interim constitution and the first democratic elections to be held the following year. He was considered a leading candidate for the position of deputy president to Mandela.

April 1993

Oliver Tambo died from a stroke and was succeeded as ANC president by Nelson Mandela.

1993

State President FW de Klerk and Nelson Mandela were jointly awarded the Nobel Peace Prize.

Did you know?

In 1993 South Africa became the first and only country to destroy its nuclear weapons arsenal.

Soweto's Vilakaze Street is the only place in the world where two Nobel Peace laureates (ex-president Nelson Mandela and Archbishop Emeritus Desmond Tutu) lived on the same street.

27 April 1994

Millions of South Africans stood in long queues to cast their votes in the country's first democratic elections. Nineteen political parties contested the elections, which was won in a landslide by the ANC. On the same day the new six-colour national flag was flown for the first time.

10 May 1994

Mandela was inaugurated as South Africa's first demo-cratically elected president.

Mandela's Inauguration Speech (1994)

We understand it still that there is no easy road to freedom. We know it well that none of us acting alone can achieve success. We must therefore act together as a united people, for national reconciliation, for nation building, for the birth of a new world. Let there be justice for all. Let there be peace for all. Let there be work, bread, water and salt for all. Let them know that for each the body, the mind and the soul have been freed to fulfil themselves. Never, never and never again shall it be that this beautiful land will again experience the oppression of one by another and suffer the indignity of being the skunk of the world. The sun shall never set on so glorious a human achievement. Let freedom reign. God bless Africa.

1995

A new constitution was adopted. One of the most progressive in the world, it recognised the rights of groups and extended equal status to 11 official languages. The Truth and Reconciliation Commission (TRC) was also established to foster unity through an understanding of the underlying causes of the brutality of the apartheid past. It was headed by Archbishop Desmond Tutu and was authorised to grant amnesty to human rights abusers who made a full disclosure of their deeds.

2 June 1999

The Nelson Mandela presidential years came to an end, and so began Thabo Mbeki's presidency.

17 December 2007

Jacob Zuma defeated Thabo Mbeki for the ANC presidency at the movement's conference held in Polokwane.

24 September 2008

Mbeki resigned as president and was succeeded in a caretaker role by Kgalema Motlanthe.

22 April 2009

South Africa conducted its fourth election since democracy, which was won by the ANC with a reduced majority.

Jacob Zuma was inaugurated as South Africa's third democratically elected president.

Best political scandals

- Willem van der Stel introduced a long tradition of sleaze to South African politics when he cornered the market in wine and meat while governor of the Cape in the early eighteenth century. He was banished to the Netherlands on 23 April 1707, making him one of the few to pay the price for corruption
- The Jameson Raid of 1896
- The Excelsior affair of 1970. One of the cruellest pieces of apartheid legislation was the Immorality Act, which outlawed sex across the colour line. Six men in the Orange Free State hamlet of Excelsior, in the heartland of National Party support, were caught with their pants down with 14 black women, which brought international embarrassment on the government. Rather than repeal the Act, however, they made it all go away by convincing the ever-pliant Attorney-General of the Free State, Dr Percy Yutar, to drop the charges 'in the interests of the country's image'
- The Info Scandal of 1978
- The Arms Deal of 1998, which has enriched many and threatened to destabilise our young democracy

Useless
INFORMATION

South Africa is situated on the southern tip of Africa and includes Marion and Prince Edward islands in the southern Atlantic. It is bordered on three sides by the cool Atlantic and warm Indian oceans. To the north and north-east it shares borders with Namibia, Botswana, Zimbabwe, Swaziland and Mozambique. Lesotho is completely contained within the country.

AREA

South Africa covers an area of 1 219 912 square kilometres, making it the 25th biggest country in the world.

LANDFORM

The country is characterised by lowlands around the 3 000-kilometre coastline, which are separated from the interior plateau by the dramatic Great Escarpment. The interior plateau with its wide plains is the end point of the African plateau that begins at the Sahara Desert.

CLIMATE

South Africa has a temperate climate, making it one of the best year-round destinations in the world. Most provinces enjoy summer rainfall, with occasional afternoon thunderstorms. Part of the Western Cape has a Mediterranean climate with winter rainfall and hot, dry summers. Snow sometimes falls on the inland plateau and mountain peaks during winter.

The country has an annual rainfall of 450 millimetres, which is just over half the world average. This, however, is not evenly spread, as most of it falls in the eastern part of the country, with some places on the Eastern Escarpment receiving over 1 200 millimetres, while the Karoo and parts of the Kalahari Desert that reach into the Northern Cape experience virtually none.

Summer is from November to February; autumn from March to April; winter from May to August; and spring from September to October. Because of the higher elevation above sea level of the interior plateau, temperatures are not as severe in summer and are cooler in winter than countries of similar latitude. Coastal climatic patterns are affected by the warm Agulhas current that runs down the east and along the south coasts and the cold Benguela that flows up the west coast. Their influences mean the east and south coasts are wetter and more humid, while the west coast is drier and windier.

GOVERNMENT

South Africa is a constitutional democracy with an entrenched Bill of Rights that ensures individual freedoms. The judiciary is independent of the state, with the highest court being the Constitutional Court that sits in Johannesburg. There are three tiers of government: national, provincial and metropolitan.

- Eastern Cape – Bisho
- Free State – Bloemfontein, which is also the judicial capital of South Africa
- Gauteng – Johannesburg, while Pretoria is the administrative capital of South Africa
- KwaZulu-Natal – Pietermaritzburg
- Limpopo – Polokwane
- Mpumalanga – Nelspruit
- Northern Cape – Kimberley
- North West – Mafikeng
- Western Cape – Cape Town, which is also the executive capital of South Africa

> The city of Pretoria falls within the greater municipal area known as Tshwane, which includes previously disadvantaged black townships. A solution offered by some groups to the ongoing name dispute for the city is a combination of the two: Pretoria / Tshwane. In this book we refer to Pretoria, as this is still most widely used.

NATIONAL SYMBOLS

The South African flag was introduced for the first democratic elections (27 April 1994) and the inauguration of Nelson Mandela as the first democratically elected president of the country (10 May 1994). Designed by State Herald Frederick Brownlee, it contains only one symbolic element in the form of the horizontal 'Y' representing the convergence of diverse cultures.

The South African Coat of Arms was adopted on 27 April 2000. The motto, '!ke e:/xarra//ke', means 'diverse people unite' in the now extinct language of the /Xam Khoisan people. Included in the design, with various symbolic meanings, are human figures taken from Bushman rock art on a shield framed by ears of wheat and elephant tusks crowned by a protea and secretary bird beneath a rising sun.

National emblems

- National animal – springbok
- National bird – blue crane
- National flower – king or giant protea
- National fish – galjoen
- National tree – yellowwood

Did you know?

The South African flag is the only one in the world with six colours and without a seal or brocade.

NATIONAL ANTHEM

Before 1994 the official South African anthem was 'Die Stem', also translated into English from Afrikaans into 'The Call of South

Africa'. It was written by CJ Langenhoven in 1918 and set to music in 1921 by the Reverend Marthinus de Villiers. Unofficially, the Xhosa hymn 'Nkosi Sikelel' iAfrika' composed by lay preacher Enoch Sontonga in 1899 became the rallying anthem of the Struggle for Freedom. After the first democratic elections the two anthems were merged, with the four verses in five of the official languages – isiXhosa, isiZulu, Sesotho, Afrikaans and English.

Nkosi sikelel' iAfrika
Maluphakanyisw' uphondo lwayo,
Yizwa imithandazo yethu,
Nkosi sikelela, thina lusapho lwayo.

Morena boloka setjhaba sa heso,
O fedise dintwa la matshwenyeho,
O se boloke, O se boloke setjhaba sa heso,
Setjhaba sa South Afrika – South Afrika.

Uit die blou van onse hemel,
Uit die diepte van ons see,
Oor ons ewige gebergtes,
Waar die kranse antwoord gee.

Sounds the call to come together,
And united we shall stand,
Let us live and strive for freedom,
In South Africa our land.

Lord, bless Africa
May her spirit rise high up,
Hear thou our prayers,

Lord bless us.
Lord, bless Africa,
Banish wars and strife,
Lord, bless our nation,
Of South Africa.

Ringing out from our blue heavens,
From our deep seas breaking round,
Over everlasting mountains,
Where the echoing crags resound.

Sounds the call to come together,
And united we shall stand,
Let us live and strive for freedom,
In South Africa our land.

Did you know?

The South African national
anthem is the only one in the
world to include five languages.
Part of it is based on Enoch
Sontonga's hymn *Nkosi Sikelel'
iAfrika*, which is also the national
anthem of Zambia.

- New Year's Day – 1 January
- Human Rights Day – 21 March (commemorates the Sharpeville Massacre of 21 March 1960)
- Good Friday – the Friday before Easter Sunday
- Family Day – the Monday after Easter Sunday
- Freedom Day – 27 April (the date of the first democratic elections in 1994)
- Worker's Day – 1 May
- Youth Day – 16 June (in remembrance of the start of the 1976 Soweto Uprising)
- National Women's Day – 9 August (recalling the march by 20 000 women on the Union Buildings in 1956 in protest against the extension of Pass Laws to black women)
- Heritage Day – 24 September (a celebration of our diverse heritage)
- Day of Reconciliation – 16 December (this used to be the Day of the Vow that celebrated the Boer defeat of the Zulu at Blood River on 16 December 1838 and was the day on which the armed wing of the African National Congress (ANC) was founded in 1961, but is now used to bring our diverse cultures together in peace).
- Christmas Day – 25 December
- Day of Goodwill – 26 December

If any of these dates falls on a Sunday, the following Monday becomes a public holiday.

Nelson Mandela's birthday, 18 July, has been proposed as a public holiday.

POPULATION

South Africa has a population of about 48 million people. It is a fully integrated society despite its turbulent past and diverse culture. Black groups make up nearly 80 per cent of the population, whites and coloureds roughly nine per cent each, with the balance of Asian origin.

The two major black groups are those of Nguni and Sotho origin. The Nguni are broadly divided into Zulu, Xhosa, Ndebele and Swazi speakers; and the Sotho into South Sotho, North Sotho (Pedi) and Tswana. Most whites are of either Dutch (Afrikaans) or British descent, with significant representation of German, French, Portuguese, Greek and Italian communities. Coloureds are people descended from slaves from the old Dutch East Indies (sometimes referred to as Cape Malays) or interracial relationships. Asians are predominantly Indian, with a sizeable Chinese component.

To give equal status to the major groups, the Constitution recognises 11 official languages: Afrikaans (spoken by people of Dutch descent and most of the coloured community), English, isiNdebele, isiXhosa, isiZulu, Sesotho sa Leboa, Sesotho, Setswana, siSwati, Tshivenda and Xitsonga. While isiZulu and isiXhosa are the most widely spoken, English is widely understood and generally used for communication between groups.

Did you know?

The word 'stranger' is unknown in any of South Africa's indigenous languages.

Khoisan

The rich Bushman or San heritage is that of the original people
of southern Africa. It is even believed that the genes of the San
Bushmen of South Africa predate the rest of humanity, making
them the original ancestors. The name Khoisan is an integration
of the two names of the first inhabitants of southern Africa, the
San and the Khoikhoi. It is a sad part of our history that these rich
tribes are almost extinct, with many pushed to the periphery of
our society. Today, there are no distinct communities of San left.
However, their 'cousins', the Bushmen, are still evident in the
Kalahari Desert, Namibia and Botswana. Khoisan communities
can still be found in Namaqualand and the Richtersveld of the
Northern Cape. But San culture lives on through their rock
art and the work of anthropologists searching for the origins of
modern man.

Did you know?

In San culture there is no concept of land ownership, leadership or private possession, which led to bitter conflict with the settlers as the San would hunt their livestock.

Zulu

The Zulu people are the 'people of the heavens'. Once a disparate group of clans and chieftainships, they were melded into a great kingdom by Shaka in the early nineteenth century. Because of the exploits of Shaka and his successors, the Zulu are arguably the most renowned group in Africa. They currently number 9,2 million people, with most living in KwaZulu-Natal. Their language, isiZulu, is the most widely spoken in South Africa.

Did you know?

The Zulu inflicted the heaviest defeat ever by an ethnic group on imperial Britain in the Battle of Isandlwana during the Anglo-Zulu War of 1879.

Xhosa

The Xhosa people are extremely proud of their heritage and their hold on many traditions remains fierce. They number approximately 7,1 million, the majority living in the Eastern Cape.

The Xhosa people are descendant from the Nguni, who migrated from central and northern Africa to settle in southern Africa. They comprise a number of clans such as Gcaleka, Ngika, Ndlambe, Dushane, Qayi and the Gqunkhwebe of Khoisan origin. Enchantment winds through the Xhosa language, dress and rituals. Their language is often called the 'click' language because of the three dominant clicks, which came about when they mixed with the Khoisan.

Did you know?

Many mariners and passengers shipwrecked along the Wild Coast in the eighteenth and nineteenth centuries were assimilated into Xhosa culture.

Sotho

It is estimated that there are 7 million Sotho people living in South Africa, which makes it the second largest African language group in the country. There are another 3 million who live outside the country, mainly in Lesotho. The Sotho people are generally broken into three groups: Southern Sotho, Northern Sotho and Tswana.

Did you know?

The Sotho clans were melded into a kingdom by King Moshoeshoe in the early nineteenth century.

Tswana

The Tswana people emerged from the larger Sotho group and today number some 2 million spread through the Northern Cape, Gauteng and North West provinces. No one is sure where the name Tswana came from or what it means.

Ndebele

Colour is the hallmark of the Ndebele people. For centuries these hospitable people, whose origins are shrouded in mystery, have used hues in their dress and mural art to tell stories of their lives. South Africa has two Ndebele groups, who are thought to have migrated from KwaZulu-Natal in the early seventeenth century. The one group is situated north-east of Johannesburg in Bronkhorstspruit, while the other resides in Limpopo Province.

Did you know?

Ndebele traditional geometric mural art is done freehand without preparatory sketches, rulers or mathematical instruments.

Swazi

The majority of Swazi people live in Swaziland, with some in Mpumalanga and urban areas within South Africa.

Shangaan-Tsonga

Tsonga people are called Shangaan, but prefer the name vhaTsonga (the Tsonga people) as they say the Shangaan are a different tribe. In truth, the Tsonga are a diverse group consisting of Shangaan, Thonga, Tonga and other smaller ethnic groups. The history of the Tsonga culture is a complex one, littered with many players. It starts in the eighteenth century when the first Tonga traders came to southern Africa to barter cloth and beads for ivory, copper and salt. Their peaceful life ended when Zulu king Shaka sent one of his commanders, Soshangane, to conquer them in Mozambique in the early nineteenth century. Soshangane did what he had been sent to do, but instead of returning decided to stay in the region and incorporated the Tsonga into his culture, thus forming the Shangaan tribe.

Did you know?

The famous gumboot dance of gold miners was started by the Shangaan-Tsonga people.

Venda

The Venda people were one of the last black groups to migrate south of the Limpopo River. When they moved into South Africa they found a beautiful, bountiful area, which they named Venda (Pleasant Place) and settled there. In Venda tradition there are many sacred sites, especially Lake Fundudzi high in the Soutspansberg Mountains. Even today, it is believed this is where the White Python – the god of fertility – lives. In reverence to the python, young female initiates perform the Domba dance, in which the girls form a chain of bodies. When they move to the rhythm of beating drums, it replicates the movement of a snake, as well as a baby in the womb.

What sets the Venda apart from other groups in South Africa is the role of art in the community. Artists are called by the spirit world in much the same way as traditional healers are, which gives their work supernatural energy.

Did you know?

The Venda king has his own language as a sign of his divinity.

Did you know?

The Venda language uses the Latin alphabet of the Lemba tribe who live among them.

Afrikaner

It is often said that the Afrikaner people are the only indigenous white tribe of Africa. Certainly, their language, Afrikaans, is the only one created in Africa for a white group of people. However, it is also spoken by most coloured people. There are approximately 3 million Afrikaners in South Africa. They have their roots embedded in their Dutch, German, Belgian and French forebears

Afrikaans is a variant of Dutch and includes elements of Malay, Portuguese, French, German and indigenous Khoi and African languages. In the nineteenth century it was recognised as a separate language, though it only replaced Dutch as an official language in 1925. The Taal Monument on Paarl Mountain commemorates Afrikaans. Paarl, though not the first place to erect an Afrikaans language monument, was chosen as the site in honour of the community's central role in getting recognition for the language. It was completed in 1975 and opened on the centenary of the founding of the Society of Real Afrikaners in the town.

Coloureds

South African coloured culture is unique to this country but is not easy to define as it refers to all people not categorised as white, black or Asian under racial classifications during apartheid.

The first coloured people of South Africa were slaves brought to the Cape by the Dutch from the Dutch East Indies. While the descendants of these people are sometimes called Cape Malays, they are broadly categorised as coloured and are mainly Muslim. The majority of South Africa's 4 million coloured people are from mixed race. Notwithstanding the country's racial policies prior to 1994, there was significant mixing across racial lines. Many live in the Western Cape and subscribe to the Christian faith.

English cultural influence began with the second British occupation of the Cape in 1806, and especially with the arrival of their first immigrants in April 1820. They also brought with them English beliefs, which were mainly rooted in the Anglican Church. With them came missionaries who worked among many of the tribes, often siding with their plight. This led to upheavals, among these the Great Trek exodus from the Cape.

To commemorate their arrival a living memorial, the 1820 Settlers Monument, was built overlooking Grahamstown in 1974. Today it hosts the annual National Arts Festival in June/July.

Did you know?

The National Arts Festival in Grahamstown is the second largest in the world after Edinburgh, offering hundreds of plays, dance presentations, art exhibitions and music concerts.

Asian

South African Indian culture began in 1860 when the first immigrants arrived on board the *Truro* as indentured labourers to work on sugar cane farms in present-day KwaZulu-Natal. Today there are about 1,2 million people of Indian descent in South Africa, with most in KwaZulu-Natal and Johannesburg.

South Africa has the largest
Indian population in the world
outside of India and the largest
Buddhist temple outside Asia at
Bronkhorstspruit in Mpumalanga.

Immigrants from Europe

South African immigrant culture has added a wonderful flavour
to the rainbow nation. Deserving first mention amongst these are
the Portuguese, as it was they who first circumnavigated Africa.
There was a steady flow of Portuguese into South Africa before
the 1970s, especially from the island of Madeira. This escalated
after the Portuguese were ousted by liberation movements from
their colonies of Mozambique and Angola. These people brought
with them the wonderful variations of their national cuisine that
was fired by the peri-peri chilli.

After the Dutch came French Huguenots fleeing religious persecution in the 1680s. They settled mainly round Franschhoek in
the Western Cape and their influence on our wine industry has
been immense. Adding to these were Germans, many of whom
still keep to their traditions in the Wartburg area of KwaZulu-
Natal. Other significant immigrant groups from Europe were the
Greeks, who brought their Mediterranean cuisine to the table,
and the Irish.

Amongst the most influential immigrants have been the Italians
and Jews. Many of the Italians were sent as prisoners of war and

remained, giving us their magnificent building skills and sublime cuisine. Most of the Jewish immigrants came with the discovery of mineral wealth and during the turmoil in Europe in the early twentieth century. They have been a potent force in making South Africa an economic powerhouse.

Without doubt the most interesting Judaic group in South Africa is the Lemba tribe of Limpopo Province. At the time of Moses they began migrating from the Middle East to eventually settle among the Venda people. They still practise Judaism, and DNA evidence has linked them to the priestly class of Israel. It is thought that it might have been their influence that shaped the walled cities of Great Zimbabwe, Mapungubwe and Thulamela.

Did you know?

The Lemba believe their ancestors brought with them the drum of the Ark of the Covenant.

Did you know?

About 300 Jewish volunteers fought alongside the Boer forces during the Anglo-Boer War of 1899-1902.

CULTURAL VILLAGES

South African cultural villages allow the visitor to step back in time to see how the people of this land once lived. Found mainly in the east of the country, most offer the additional benefit of overnight accommodation. Some of these celebrate the ethnic diversity of the country, while others focus on the traditions of one group.

Best cultural villages

- Shangana Cultural Village outside Hazyview in Mpumalanga – set amongst ancient trees, it is a celebration of a fascinating people
- Shakaland between Eshowe and Melmoth in Zululand – a taste of the richness of Zulu culture
- Ndebele Open-Air Museum at the Historical Village of Botshabelo outside Middleburg in Mpumalanga – aesthetically pleasing without the kitsch of other cultural villages

Give a wide berth to

- Lesedi Cultural Village outside Johannesburg – a tourist trap
- The one at Sun City – a crummy theme park within a crummy theme park

RELIGION

South African religious freedom is safeguarded by the Constitution. While the state is secular, only major Christian holidays are officially observed as the population is overwhelmingly Christian. Every major traditional Christian denomination is represented in the country, with the largest being the Dutch Reformed churches that are rooted in Calvinism. This is followed by the Roman Catholic, Methodist, Anglican, Lutheran, Presbyterian and Congregationalist churches.

There are also a range of churches representing immigrant communities from Greek Orthodox to Rastafarian. Since the 1960s there has been a large movement towards charismatic churches, with the largest being Rhema in Randburg.

Christianity includes the African Independent Churches. There are a vast array of these, and an even greater number of sects. With over 5 million adherents, the Zionist Christian Church (ZCC) based at Moria near Polokwane is the single largest congregation in the country. This is followed closely by Apostolic and Pentecostal offshoots of various missionary orders.
One of the most colourful of the African Independent Churches is the Shembe of KwaZulu-Natal. Their pilgrimages, ceremonies and celebrations offer a compelling convergence of biblical teachings with traditional African ancestor worship, dance, polygamy and coming-of-age ceremonies.

There are also sizeable adherents to Islam, Hinduism and Buddhism across South Africa. Hindu temples are found mainly in Johannesburg and Durban, which also has the largest mosque in the southern hemisphere. South Africa also boasts the largest Buddhist temple outside Asia at Bronkhorstspruit in Mpumalanga.

Jewish temples can be found in all major centres.

African ancestor worship, the predominant pre-colonial belief system across most of sub-Saharan Africa, is the veneration of deceased family members. This is not the same as mourning or remembering the dead, but the belief that spirits continue to take an interest in the affairs of the living and possess the ability to influence events. This belief system is not uniquely African, however. It is found across the world from Asia and Europe to native American culture in the US and Canada. Common to all these is the importance of ensuring the continued well-being of those who have passed on, so they in turn will respond positively when intervention is required.

An important aspect of ancestral belief is the role of the sangoma or traditional healer, who plays a central role in the health and spiritual well-being of the community. They are the interpreters through whom the ancestors and the living communicate. The ancestor can also appear to the family member in dreams, but only the sangoma can decipher the meaning.

Churches

The history of churches in South Africa stretches back to the arrival of Dutch settlers at the Cape in 1652. They brought with them the Dutch Reformed faith and in 1665 built the first of the South African churches, the Groote Kerk (Great Church) in central Cape Town. This remains the most important Dutch Reformed church in the country, notable also for its enormous organ that with 5 917 pipes is the largest in the country.

Each new Dutch settlement was established around an imposing church, most of which remain and are the first thing the visitor sees when approaching a town. Churches became more diverse with the arrival of other settlers, especially the British. Grahamstown has so many churches that it is known as the City of Saints.

Among the more interesting around the country are the Italian Prisoner of War Church in Pietermaritzburg and the 1820 Settler Scottish Memorial Church in the Eastern Cape where missionary Thomas Pringle is buried. Surely the most eccentric is the Sir Herbert Baker-designed Church of St John the Baptist outside Vaalwater, which holds barely 20 people. But arguably the most famous South African churches are those that were at the forefront of the Struggle for Freedom. The most notable of these are the Cathedral Church of St George the Martyr in Cape Town; the Anglican Church of Christ the King in Sophiatown; the Central Methodist Church in Johannesburg; and Regina Mundi, the largest Catholic Church in Soweto, which still has bullet holes in the walls from the time of the Soweto uprisings in 1976 when police stormed the church and fired at fleeing students.

Did you know?

The Anglican Church of Christ the King was the only building left standing by the apartheid authorities when they forcibly removed the residents of Sophiatown in Johannesburg.

South African kramats and mosques are an important part of our heritage as they represent the second oldest religion introduced to the country.

The first Muslims brought to the Cape arrived as Malay slaves, who practised their faith in secret until the early nineteenth century. Also brought to the Cape were prisoners fighting for freedom in the Dutch East Indies. Among these were teachers of Islam, or Auliyah. Some of these holy men were also of noble birth and those who died here were buried in shrines known as kramats or mazaars, of which there are about 30 in a circle in and around Cape Town.

Kramats, which resemble miniature mosques, can be found from Muizenberg to Mowbray with four on Signal Hill. The most visited by pilgrims is that of Sheikh Yusuf of Macassar in the dunes near Macassar Beach. He was the first to read from the Holy Koran in South Africa and is regarded as the father of local Islam. Other important kramats are those of the last Malaccan sultan, Sheikh Abdurahman Matebe Shahnat, at the gates to Klein Constantia and of Sheikh Sayed Abdurahman Maturu of Jafet on Robben Island.

ECONOMY

South Africa is a leading developing economy with a well-established formal sector operating side-by-side with a vibrant informal component. While the economy today is broadly based, it was founded on our rich mineral deposits that still play a prominent role.

Did you know?

The Witwatersrand Gold Fields are estimated to be 30 times richer than any other gold fields in the world.

Trivia in our economic development

- The Star of South Africa diamond was found in 1869 near Hopetown in the Northern Cape. It was an 83,5 carat crystal and the diamond cut from it 47,69 carats. It was purchased and cut by Louis Hond and sold to the Earl of Dudley. Countess Dudley wore it as a hair ornament and it today resides in the Natural History Museum in London.
- The richest ever deposit of diamonds was found at Colesberg Kopje on 16 July 1871. This led to the birth of Kimberley and the start of the industrialisation of southern Africa. Today Kimberley is an elegant city with a strong tourism sector focusing on diamonds and their turbulent history.

Did you know?

The Big Hole in Kimberley, once where Colesberg Kopje stood, is the largest hand-dug excavation in the world.

- Gold was discovered in 1881 near Sabie in the foothills of the Eastern Escarpment of what is now Mpumalanga.
- Gold was discovered on the Witwatersrand by Australian prospector George Harrison on 24 July 1886. It heralded a rush of fortune seekers that swamped the local Boer population. With them came blacks and coloureds in search of work. Within months the landscape was strewn with wagons and tents organised in camps along streams and interconnected by a wagon trail that would later become Commissioner Street. And so Johannesburg was born.
- The discovery of gold led to the formation of a permanent newspaper industry in South Africa in February 1887. Within six months there were three newspapers servicing the mining camp – the *Digger's News*, *Witwatersrand Advertiser* and *Transvaal Mining Argus*, which all appeared within a day of each other. Others came and went, of which only the *Eastern Star*, which was to become *The Star*, survived.
- In 1888 Cecil John Rhodes formed De Beers Consolidated Mines, which at one time controlled over 90 per cent of the world's trade in uncut diamonds.
- The Cullinan diamond was unearthed at the Premier Mine at Cullinan in Gauteng on 26 January 1905. At 3 106 carats, it remains the largest diamond ever found.

Did you know?

The diamond cut from the Cullinan diamond is known as the Great Star of Africa and is set in the Imperial State Crown.

- Wall Street crashed on what came to be known as Black Thursday on 24 October 1929, culminating in the Great Depression. While South Africa was not as badly affected as the US or Europe, exports fell, jobs were lost and wages slashed. Hardest hit were blacks, who were the first to be made redundant. Soup kitchens proliferated and work colonies for public service works were established for the white destitute. Matters were exacerbated in 1933 by one of the worst droughts on record.
- The South African Atomic Energy Board was constituted in 1949.
- Aaron Klug, who was raised in South Africa, won the Nobel Prize for Chemistry in 1982. He now lives in Cambridge.
- Mark Shuttleworth became the first South African and second civilian in space in April 2002. Having made a fortune from the sale of his information technology company, Thawte Consulting, he paid $20 million to a Russian aerospace agency for the experience in a Soyuz TM-34 spacecraft.

Currency

The South African decimal currency, the rand, replaced the British currency on 'R-day', 14 February 1961. Then R2 would have bought you £1 or $2, showing just how expensive apartheid was.

HEALTH

The disparities between rich and poor are no more evident than in the South African health system. On one side is a fantastic academic tradition that has produced some of the great medical minds and fine private healthcare and on the other a deeply dysfunctional public hospital system that appears beyond repair. The latter can be ascribed to apartheid and a misguided President Thabo Mbeki. This anomaly is not just in hospitals, but everywhere. For example, South Africa is one of a dozen countries in the world with tap water fit to drink, but which annually loses citizens to cholera.

Medical trivia

- In 1951 Pretoria-born Max Theiler became the first South African to win a Nobel Prize for his discoveries regarding yellow fever. Most of his work was done in the US.
- Dr Christiaan Neethling Barnard, who had researched ways of revolutionising cardiac surgery, performed the first successful heart transplant on Louis Washkansky at Cape Town's Groote Schuur Hospital on 2 December 1967. The donor was 25-year-old Denise Darvall, who was killed along with her mother as they crossed Main Road in Observatory. The recipient survived for 18 days before succumbing to pneumonia.
- South African-born Allan Cormack won the Nobel Prize for Medicine for the development of computer-assisted tomography in 1979. Most of his work was done in the US.
- Germiston-born Sydney Brenner won a Nobel Prize in 2002 for his discovery concerning genetic regulation of organ development and programmed cell death. Most of his research was done in the UK and US.

South Africa has a well-developed communications infrastructure, with extensive landline phone networks and a number of cell-phone service providers offering national coverage.

Communications trivia

- South African resident Alfred Jennings in 1896 discovered the coherer, which detects electronic waves and is used in wireless telegraphy.
- The first definitive South African stamps, showing the profile of King George V, were issued in 1913.

Did you know?

Our first post office was a tree, which is now a national monument. Known as the Post Office Tree, it is in Mossel Bay and was used by early seafarers under which to leave letters.

TRANSPORTATION

More than 10 000 people die each year on South Africa's roads. That is nearly 27 people per 100 000. Most of these are pedestrians, but a large portion is from taxi-related accidents.

- The British East Indiaman *Grosvenor* sank off the Wild Coast on 4 August 1782.

- On 26 February 1852 the troopship *HMS Birkenhead*, an iron paddle-steamer, sank along the Cape South Coast. This incident entered seafaring lore as soldiers helped women and children onto lifeboats before forming up on deck to go down with the ship to the beat of a drum. It is, however, myth that the *Birkenhead* established the practice of 'women and children first'. This honour actually goes to the *Abercrombie Robinson*, which sank in Table Bay a decade earlier. In fact, the Cape South Coast is more notorious for dishonour in shipping. When the *Jacaranda* cargo ship ran aground there in 1971, it is alleged that the captain was in his cabin with a prostitute while his drunken crew were all incapacitated, save for a 16-year-old at the helm. Two decades later the captain and most of the crew of the *Oceanos* abandoned ship and passengers when the Greek liner foundered in the same waters, leaving it to the South African entertainment staff to avert tragedy.

- The first rail tracks in South Africa were laid in Cape Town on 31 March 1859 and in September the first steam locomotive arrived in the city. But the Natal Locomotive Company was the first with an operational train in Durban on 26 June 1860. By July 1937 the country had an extensive rail network when the internationally renowned luxury Blue Train was launched.

- The worst rail disaster in South Africa was the Braamfontein dynamite tragedy of 19 February 1896. Most of the casualties were from surrounding suburbs. The dubious distinction of a train wreck claiming the greatest number of passengers belongs to Train 513, carrying mine-workers home from the Witwatersrand to Mozambique on 15 November 1949, which crashed on the Elands River Bridge between Waterval Boven and Waterval Onder in Mpumalanga.

- The first electric tram in South Africa ran between Adderley Street and Mowbray Hill in Cape Town on 6 August 1896. Over the next 14 years, all the major centres followed suit. These began to be replaced 35 years later by electrified double-decker trackless trams that used the overhead booms of the tramcars.

- The first motorcar in South Africa, a 1½ hp Benz Voiturette imported by John Hess, was shown at Berea Park in Pretoria where it circled a cycle track on 4 January 1897. Five years later the first motorcycle appeared in the country.

- The Voisin of visiting French aviator Albert Kimmerling lifted six metres above East London's Nahoon Racecourse for South Africa's first flight on 28 December 1909. A decade later Major Allister Miller, a distinguished World War I pilot, inaugurated South African Aerial Transport, the first airline to operate in the country. Its successor, Union Airways, was taken over by the government in 1934 and renamed South African Airways (SAA).

Did you know?

The first wholly built South African aircraft, piloted by John Weston, took to the skies above Kimberley in 1911.

- South African Railways and Harbours was established in 1910.
- South African aviators Pierre van Ryneveld and Quintin Brand completed the first flight from Britain to South Africa in 1920.
- SAA's first accident was on 16 June 1937, when a Junkers crashed at Port Elizabeth Airport. The first with fatalities was when a Lockheed crashed at Elands Bay on 28 March 1941, when all on board were killed. In all there have been 10 accidents involving the national carrier.
- Bob van Niekerk, Willie Meissner and Verster de Wit in 1956 built the prototype for South Africa's first car, the GSM Dart, which went on to successfully compete on the racetracks of the world. However, there was little local demand and production ceased in 1965.
- The only hijacking to involve an SAA aircraft took place on 24 May 1972 on a flight between what is now Harare in Zimbabwe and Johannesburg. The two Lebanese nationals who took control of the plane did so over a dispute with the Oppenheimers, believing a family member would be on board.
- On 27 November 1987, Flight SA295 crashed in the Indian Ocean. The SAA Boeing 747, *The Helderberg*, was carrying 159 people, including crew. It is the country's worst air disaster. The cause of the crash remains controversial.

Did you know?

Durban's harbour is the busiest in South Africa and one of the 10 largest worldwide.

Best drives in South Africa

- The Garden Route
- The circular drive from Cape Town through Muizenberg to Cape Point and back via Noordhoek
- The Chapman's Peak drive between Noordhoek and Hout Bay
- Umtata to Port St Johns through the Transkei countryside
- The Valley of a Thousand Hills in KwaZulu-Natal
- The passes of the Western Cape, especially Bain's Kloof, Swartberg and Montagu
- Sani Pass in KwaZulu-Natal
- South to north through the Kruger National Park
- The R532 from Graskop to the Echo Caves in Mpumalanga
- The R71 or R528 from Tzaneen to Haenertsburg in Limpopo
- The Maloti Route from Bethlehem to Ladybrand in the eastern Free State
- Route 62 through the Klein Karoo

CRIME AND OCCASIONAL PUNISHMENT

South Africa abolished capital punishment on 7 June 1995, when the Constitutional Court ruled the practice did not accord with the Bill of Rights. The last person executed was Solomon Ngobeni on 14 November 1989. However, there were two further executions after this in the nominally independent homelands of Bophuthatswana and Venda when Alpheus Sekoboane and John Tsakani Chauke were put to death on 12 November 1990 and 31

Smith on 2 June 1989. It is thought that the last public execution
was of Henry Nicholls in Grahamstown on 19 February 1862.

Did you know?

Only intense international
pressure saved Nelson Mandela
and others from being sentenced
to death at the conclusion of the
Rivonia Trial in 1964.

South Africa's first recorded mass murderer was Pierre Basson,
who in the early twentieth century killed eight or nine people,
including his brother Jasper. The first recorded spree killing was
by Stephanus Swart in Charlestown on 6 May 1927, when he ran
amok and killed nine people and injured three before turning
the gun on himself. The most infamous, however, was on 15
November 1988, when Barend Strydom shot dead eight black
people in a racist attack in Strydom Square in Pretoria.

South Africa's first serial killer, and most infamous, was Daisy
de Melker, who was accused of murdering two husbands and her
son for insurance payouts. She was only convicted of her son's
murder, however, and was executed on 30 December 1932. Other
serial killers were the Loskop Murderer, who killed nine people,
mostly Indian shopkeepers, between 1929 and 1936; the Wemmer
Pan Killer, who murdered at least 27 people; and the Phoenix
Strangler, who raped and murdered 19 women in the late 1990s.
The worst serial killer was Moses Sitole, who raped and murdered
at least 38 women in the mid-1990s. He is serving a 2 410-year
prison term.

Among the most sensational unsolved murders in South Africa were of Bubbles Schroeder on 16 August 1949 and Dr Robert Smit and his wife in 1977. Three sons of prominent Johannesburg Jewish families were charged with the murder of 'good-time girl' Schroeder, but were acquitted. Smit was the South African representative to the International Monetary Fund and a National Party candidate in the forthcoming elections and it is believed he had details of a secret Swiss bank account in the name of former state president Nico Diedrichs. No one was ever charged for this murder, though it is suspected to have been carried out by the infamous Bureau of State Security. And while there is doubt as to whether the incident was an accident or crime, there is strong suspicion that Mozambican president Samora Machel was in some way assassinated by the apartheid regime when his plane crashed on 19 October 1986 in the Lebombo Mountains of Mpumalanga.

Historic

ATTRACTIONS

South African historical museums cover nearly every aspect of life. With the country's history stretching back to the dawn of humankind and born in cataclysm, our past is reflected in our monuments and historical buildings, all telling of the diverse influences on our heritage.

More than 300 museums are spread across the country, from the smallest towns to the largest cities. National museums include the South African and Robben Island museums in Cape Town; the National and Anglo-Boer War museums in Bloemfontein; the National Cultural History Museum and Transvaal Museum of Natural History in Pretoria; and the National Museum of Military History in Johannesburg. The last three comprise the National Flagship Institution.

There are many national monuments and memorials commemorating those who shaped who we are. Some of these, such as Robben Island, are World Heritage Sites, while others point to the quirky side of our character.

Among the national memorials are the Huguenot Monument in Franschhoek, dedicated to the French religious refugees who settled at the Cape in the late seventeenth century, and the National Women's Monument in Bloemfontein, which honours the thousands of women and children who succumbed in the concentration camps during the Anglo-Boer War of 1899-1902.

Provincial monuments and memorials celebrate everything from battles and the arrival of the British settlers in 1820 to hyena traps and temples. In Port Elizabeth there is the only monument in the world to Prester John, the mythical priest thought to be the key to vast African wealth and the inspiration for fifteenth-century Portuguese exploration.

In Mossel Bay you'll find the first post office in South Africa – a tree. In 1500 a Portuguese captain left a letter in an iron pot under a milkwood, which was found and delivered by a Dutch naval commander the following year. It is now a national monument known as the Post Office Tree.

Then there are the historical buildings. Ruins of early South African architecture can be seen at places like Mapungubwe and Thulamela in Limpopo. The oldest building still in use is the Castle of Good Hope in Cape Town, which was first occupied in the 1670s. But there are magnificent buildings in every part of the country, and in some of the most surprising places. Most of these are national monuments or heritage buildings, and as such cannot be altered or demolished.

Western Cape

South African Museum and Planetarium

The South African Museum and Planetarium, founded in 1825, focuses on natural history and human sciences. Set in the beautiful Company Gardens in central Cape Town, it is the oldest museum in the country. It is now part of Iziko Museums of Cape Town.

These include Slave Lodge, Koopmans-De Wet House, Bertram House, Groot Constantia, Bo-Kaap Museum, Rust en Vreugt and the William Fehr Collection in the Castle of Good Hope.

Did you know?

Using a Minolta star machine and multiple projectors, the Planetarium at the South African Museum can recreate a clear night sky regardless of the weather outside.

Castle of Good Hope

The Castle of Good Hope in Cape Town is the oldest building still in use in South Africa.

Shortly after Jan van Riebeeck arrived in 1652, he built an earthen-walled fort near the shore in the vicinity of what is now the Grand Parade. But this was inadequate to protect the passage to India of the Dutch East India Company and famous Dutch architect Menno van Coehoorn was commissioned to design a large stone castle. A site was chosen and cleared in 1665, and construction under the supervision of engineer Pieter Dombaer commenced on 2 January 1666. Even though the Castle was only completed in 1679, the garrison took occupation in 1674.

It is the best preserved of all the Dutch East India Company castles and it was declared a national monument in 1936. It was extensively renovated during the 1980s and today is the Western Cape headquarters of the South African Army.

Did you know?

The Castle of Good Hope is the most haunted building in South Africa.

Rhodes Memorial

The Rhodes Memorial on the slopes of Devil's Peak in Cape Town honours one of the most controversial figures of South Africa's past. Those who loved Cecil John Rhodes thought him a colossus; those who loathed him believed he had aspirations to be 'the Emperor of Africa'. What cannot be argued is that he was a larger-than-life character bestriding our political landscape who did much to shape the current borders of southern Africa.

Designed by esteemed architect Herbert Baker, it is situated on Rhodes' favourite spot facing north-east, on land he owned on the lower slopes of Table Mountain, much of which he bequeathed to the nation on his death. Sharing space with it on parts of his old grounds are the University of Cape Town's upper campus and Kirstenbosch National Botanical Garden.

The District Six Museum

The District Six Museum moved to the old Methodist Mission Church in Buitenkant Street in Cape Town in September 2000. Now multi-media techniques add a new dimension by combining documentary, digital and sound elements to narrate the story of District Six, from which coloured residents were forcibly removed after 1966, when it was declared a white area.

Robben Island Museum

The Robben Island Museum, in what was once the political prison, is now a 'cultural and conservation showcase for the new South African democracy' – an international icon of the triumph of good over evil.

See World Heritage Sites, p 114.

Nobel Square

Nobel Square at the Victoria & Alfred Waterfront in Cape Town is a celebration of South Africa's four Nobel Peace Prize winners. While our citizens have won many other Nobel Prizes from literature to medicine, it is the peace laureates who so shaped our long walk to freedom.

The late Chief Albert Luthuli was born in 1898 and became ANC president in 1952, just when the worst aspects of apartheid policies were being implemented. It was also a difficult time within the organisation as competing groups tried to assert their influence. During his presidency the ANC adopted the Freedom Charter, but split a few years later in 1959 when Africanist elements under Robert Sobukwe refused to accept what they saw as the inclusionary nature of the organisation. Banned and jailed on numerous occasions, Luthuli received the Nobel Peace Prize in 1960. He died in mysterious circumstances in 1967.

Archbishop Desmond Tutu was born in Klerksdorp in 1931. He trained as a schoolteacher, but in 1958 decided to enter the ministry. A staunch opponent of apartheid, he was Secretary-General of the South African Council of Churches when he was awarded the Nobel Peace Prize in 1984. Two years later he became the first black person to lead the Anglican Church in South Africa.

Then state president FW de Klerk and future president Nelson Mandela were joint recipients in 1993. On 2 February 1990 De Klerk unbanned the ANC and numerous other organisations, freed Nelson Mandela and other political prisoners and entered negotiations for a new South Africa. They were honoured for their work in advancing democracy and reconciliation.

The sculptures of the four recipients were sculpted by artists Noria Mabasa and Claudette Schreuders and unveiled on 16 December 2005, the Day of Reconciliation.

Northern Cape

Kimberley Mine Museum

The Kimberley Mine Museum recaptures the diamond-frenzy days of the city. Along its cobbled streets are recreations of typical houses, a church, the Perilly tobacconist shop famed for its hand-made cigarettes, Diggers' Rest pub, the Barney Barnarto Boxing Academy, a funeral parlour and the rail carriage used by directors of De Beers. There is a lookout over the Big Hole, which is 225 metres deep with a surface area of 17 hectares and perimeter of 1,6 kilometres. The De Beers Hall in the grounds houses a display of jewellery and uncut diamonds, including a replica of the first diamond found in South Africa, the Eureka, a 23,25 carat stone found at Hopetown. There is a coffee shop here, where light meals are served.

Eastern Cape

The Red Location Museum

Situated in the New Brighton Township of Port Elizabeth, this spectacular L-shaped facility is one of the finest Struggle for Freedom sites in South Africa and has deservedly won three major international awards. Surrounded by original housing from the establishment of the township in the early 1900s, it represents the past through installations that draw powerfully on the notion of memory.

Nelson Mandela Museum

The Nelson Mandela Museum in the Transkei region of the Eastern Cape, opened on 11 February 2000, is a living memorial to this Struggle legend. It focuses on three sites: at the impressive Bhunga building in Umtata the story of his life is celebrated in his own words alongside gifts he received during his presidency; at Mvezo visitors can see where he was born; and at Qunu, the cultural village where he was raised, a youth and heritage centre is being built.

South African liberation and international peace icon Nelson Rolihlahla Mandela was born of Tembu royal lineage at Mvezo in the Eastern Cape on 18 July 1918. Arriving in Johannesburg in the early 1940s, he enrolled at UNISA to complete his law degree started at the University of Fort Hare. He joined the African National Congress (ANC) and in August 1943 took part in his first march in support of the Alexandra bus boycott. Soon the youthful Mandela was pushing to the front of resistance marches. He was also at the forefront of changing the direction of the ANC.

He was instrumental in establishing the movement's Youth League in 1944 and its armed wing, Umkhonto we Sizwe (MK), after it was forced underground. In 1963, while serving a three-year sentence for leaving the country illegally and inciting workers to strike, he was charged with treason and sentenced to life in prison. Mandela was released on 11 February 1990 and played a pivotal role in South Africa's peaceful transition, becoming the country's first democratically elected president in 1994. For his efforts he was awarded the Nobel Peace Prize.

Steve Biko Memorial

The Steve Biko Memorial in Ginsberg, a township of King Williams Town in the Eastern Cape, is dedicated to the founder of the Black Consciousness (BC) movement in South Africa.

Bantu Steven Biko was born on 18 December 1946 in Ginsberg and in 1966 enrolled at the Wentworth School of Medicine in Durban. At the time the internal struggle against apartheid was led by the white-dominated National Union of South African Students (NUSAS), which he joined. Black liberals broke away from NUSAS and launched the Black Consciousness-inspired South African Students' Organisation (SASO) in July 1969. In

1972 this became part of the larger Black People's Convention (BPC) – the political arm of BC, with Biko as its spokesman.

Inspired by the American Black Power movement, BC's philosophy was that the struggle could only be realised if blacks took control of their destiny and stopped feeling inferior to other races. This immediately struck a chord with black scholars and students, which culminated in the Soweto Uprising that began on 16 June 1976. This led to a vicious crackdown by the apartheid government, who arrested Biko and many others. On 12 September 1977 he died of injuries inflicted during a beating by security police. Today, his legacy is kept alive by the Steve Biko Foundation (SBF), which promotes a culture of South Africans becoming the architects of their future.

Did you know?

Cry Freedom, the book by Donald Woods and film by Richard Attenborough, is based on the life of Steve Biko.

Gauteng

Transvaal Museum of Natural History

The Transvaal Museum of Natural History in Pretoria, founded in 1892 as the State Museum of the Transvaal Republic, is today part of the Northern Flagship Institution, which includes the National Cultural History Museum (African Window) in Pretoria and the South African National Museum for Military History in Johannesburg.

From the outset this museum's collecting policy focused on cultural and natural history. It achieved international prominence when the slightly eccentric Dr Robert Broom was appointed palaeontologist. On 18 April 1947 he found an almost perfect adult apeman skull at Sterkfontein Caves near Johannesburg. Nicknamed Mrs Ples, this fossil, which provided evidence of the existence of apemen and the origins of humans, is now housed at this museum.

Origins Centre

The best place to get an appreciation of the San people is at the world-class Origins Centre at the University of the Witwatersrand in Johannesburg. It is a place that more than fulfils its motto to show 'We are who we are because of who we were'. Using cutting-edge technology combined with works by South Africa's foremost artists, this museum is the only one in the world to depict the evolution of humans alongside the development of their creative genius.

South African National Museum of Military History

The South African National Museum of Military History is situated in the Johannesburg suburb of Saxonwold behind the zoo. Opened on 27 August 1947, it contains over 44 000 objects arranged into 37 categories including war art, uniforms and medals. It also curates and provides the exhibits for the Delville Wood Commemorative Museum in France.

The aviation collection has the only night fighter version still in existence of the Messerschmitt Me 262 B-la/UI, the world's first operational jet-powered fighter aircraft.

African Window

The National Cultural History Museum in Pretoria, also known as the African Window, is rightly regarded as the most dynamic, innovative heritage institution in South Africa. At first part of the State Museum of the old Transvaal Republic, it moved to its own premises near the National Zoological Gardens in Boom Street in 1904. Here it became the Pretoria Museum, then the Transvaal Museum.

When the South African Mint moved premises to Midrand, the museum moved to the Old Mint building in Visagie Street. There it became the National Cultural History Museum before completely reinventing itself as the cutting-edge African Window. The museum still has its massive collection of documents, manuscripts, records, photographs and artefacts representing the country's diverse cultures and history, some of which are on permanent display. These go from the Stone and Iron Ages through our recent past to the present, including a gallery of paintings and sculptures over time.

Museum Afrika

Museum Afrika is at the heart of the Newtown Cultural Hub, an initiative to revitalise the inner city of Johannesburg. Much of the story of the city is told through its exhibits. One of the more fascinating installations is the Treason Trial section, which takes the visitor to the heart of the Struggle for Freedom. It is currently repositioning itself as a cultural history facility. It wants to use its 850 000 items to answer the question: 'What is Africa, African art and culture?' This will be based around its large collection of Bushman material, contemporary art and African cultural products.

Voortrekker Monument

The monolithic Voortrekker Monument atop Monument Hill is one of the first things a visitor sees as they drive into Pretoria from the south. It commemorates the epic exodus by disillusioned Boers from the Cape into the interior over 150 years ago, which laid the foundation for the borders of present-day South Africa.

This monument, opened on 16 December 1949, was designed by Gerard Moerdijk. Ringed by 64 granite ox wagons, it features inside the Great Hall a historical frieze and cenotaph, which is lit every 16 December by a shaft of sunlight through an opening in the roof. Outside are five massive statues of Boer leaders and another by Anton von Wouw of a Boer woman and her two children.

Did you know?

The Voortrekker Monument's granite frieze, depicting the heroics of the trekkers on 27 bas-relief panels, is the largest in the world.

Burning Truth

The Gandhi memorial, Burning Truth, outside the Hamidia Mosque in Fordsburg was created by Usha Seejarim. It depicts a cauldron, symbolic of the one Gandhi led protestors to on 16 August 1908 to burn registration cards as part of his passive resistance campaign.

Mohandas (Mahatma) Gandhi was born in India and studied law in London. In 1893 he headed for the British colony of Natal to take up a position as an advisor to a Durban law firm. Here arrangements had been made for him to travel by train to Pretoria to observe a trial. He had only intended to spend a year in South Africa, but the racial sleights he experiences on that journey were so formative that he stayed for 20.

In 1894 he founded the Natal Indian Congress, which would later be at the forefront of the Struggle for Freedom. At first it utilised passive resistance, but when this proved inadequate he reformulated it into Satyagraha, Sanskrit for 'truth and firmness'. In 1903 he began the weekly *Indian Opinion*, which focused on issues affecting this marginalised section of the community. He organised strikes and led marches to protest the Immigration Act compelling registration of Indian immigrants. Coming in for particular attention was the registration cards they were forced to carry.

Spearheading a seven-year campaign of strikes and the burning of registration cards, Gandhi was jailed on a number of occasions. While the government was able to violently quell this resistance, their methods caused an outcry, forcing them to negotiate concessions with him. Conditional on this, though, was his leaving the country and he returned to India in 1914.

Did you know?

Mahatma Gandhi was the first lawyer of colour to be admitted to the Supreme Court in South Africa.

Kliptown

Apartheid heaped indignity as well as repression upon people of colour. This was fertile ground for the ANC Youth League, which appealed in particular to the hundreds of thousands of educated urban black youths. To counter white repression, it advocated a passive resistance Plan of Action. As the campaign escalated, so repressive measures intensified.

To give the ANC a clear vision its Cape leader, Professor ZK Matthews, proposed a national convention of progressive movements from all sectors of South Africa 'to draw up a Freedom Charter for a democratic South Africa of the future'. The response was approximately 3 000 delegates, calling themselves the Congress of the People, meeting on a dusty field in Kliptown, Soweto, on 25 and 26 June 1955 to draw up the charter.

Sharpeville Human Rights Precinct

The Sharpeville Human Rights Precinct, in the Vereeniging township of Sharpeville, is a memorial to victims of apartheid brutality and a reminder to all of our rights as human beings.

Differences within the ANC following the signing of the Freedom Charter led to Robert Sobukwe breaking away to form the Pan Africanist Congress (PAC) in 1959. A year before the ANC had launched an anti-pass campaign targeting the most hated symbol of apartheid, which annually made criminals of up to half a million black people. The ANC organised a defiance campaign against passes to commence on 31 March 1960. The PAC refused to participate and called its own protest for 21 March. That Monday over 300 people marched on the police station in Sharpeville to hand in their pass books. 'Sixty-nine Africans were shot dead and at least 180 wounded when police opened fire,' reported *The World*.

Protests flared across South Africa and an outraged international community censured the country at the United Nations (UN). On 8 April, to stem the panic, the government declared a state of emergency and banned the ANC and PAC, which both went underground and established armed wings. In 1966 the UN declared 21 March the International Day for the Elimination of Racial Discrimination and since the first democratic elections in South Africa it is remembered as Human Rights Day.

Constitution Hill

Constitution Hill is a human rights precinct and a world-class heritage tourist attraction incorporating cultural, historical, artistic, educational and recreational spaces that celebrate South Africa's ability to negotiate a peaceful, miraculous democracy out of bloody oppression. It is also the home of the South African Constitutional Court, which was opened on 21 March 2004. It is located between Braamfontein and Hillbrow in Johannesburg and retains important national and international heritage buildings, including the Old Fort complex, Section 4 and 5 (Native Gaol) and the Women's Prison.

With its four lookout towers, the Old Fort was once a place of fear and hopelessness. Built by the Transvaal government in 1899 to protect the city against the advancing British during the Anglo-Boer War, it was converted in 1904 into a jail that for most of the century would house a variety of prisoners of all races. It was also the place where political prisoners were sent, including Nelson Mandela and Mahatma Gandhi, which led to it being dubbed the 'Robben Island of Johannesburg'. This is why it occupies such an indelible place in the consciousness of the nation.

The museum section of Constitution Hill includes the Mandela Cell, which features a documentary of his incarceration and emotional return 40 years later. Bricks from portions of the Old Fort that were demolished were used for the construction of the inner walls of the Constitutional Court. This is in stark contrast to the vibrant African art exhibited in the ultra-modern, low building separated from Number Four by the Great African Steps that descend to an open space incorporating sports fields.

Did you know?

The Old Fort was once the prison of both Nelson Mandela and Mahatma Gandhi.

Liliesleaf Farm

Liliesleaf Farm was for many years a meeting place and hide-out for top ANC and South African Communist Party (SACP) personnel. It is widely regarded as the birthplace of Umkhonto we Sizwe (MK), and was the site of the infamous police raid that resulted in the Rivonia Trials and eventual incarceration of many senior ANC leaders, including Nelson Mandela (who was not arrested in the raid), Govan Mbeki, Ahmed Kathrada, Raymond Mhlaba and Walter Sisulu.

The SACP bought the farm in August 1961 to use as a headquarters for their efforts against the apartheid regime. At the same time, the ANC was moving its emphasis away from passive resistance and beginning to focus more on an armed struggle. The Goldreich family moved in to masquerade as the white owners of the property and Nelson Mandela himself lived here while posing as a cook-cum-gardener under the name of David Motsamayi.

The police raid took place on 11 July 1963. It had been decided that this meeting would be the last for the MK founders at the farm, as there were fears that the security of the location had been compromised. As it turned out, these fears were well-founded as the police gained possession of the plan for the armed struggle.

Did you know?

Nelson Mandela was already in prison when the Liliesleaf police raid took place.

The Hector Peterson Museum

The Hector Peterson Museum in Soweto is a short way from where police opened fire on students on 16 June 1976.

Soon after coming to power in 1948, the National Party introduced Bantu Education, which was appallingly sub-standard. Black children, however, flocked to schools as they had a motive transcending education – the opportunity for sharing of ideas for liberation. These hot ideas were inflamed by the authorities' misguided attempts to make it compulsory for black schools to teach half the subjects in Afrikaans – an issue that was to mobilise decisive resistance. On the frosty morning of Wednesday, 16 June, scholars in Soweto assembled in school grounds before beginning their march to Orlando Stadium where a protest against Afrikaans was to be held.

On the way, not far from Phefeni Junior Secondary School on Vilikazi Street, schoolboy Hector Peterson joined a group of several thousand scholars. After a brief standoff, police opened fire on them, killing him. All hell broke loose, unleashing the Soweto Uprising. It was the single most important moment in South African history as it effectively killed the dream of grand apartheid.

Did you know?

Hastings Ndlovu, a Soweto student leader, was the first person killed during the Soweto Uprising and not Hector Peterson.

The Apartheid Museum

The Apartheid Museum, adjacent to Gold Reef City in Johannesburg, documents the Struggle for Freedom during the darkest days of racial oppression in South Africa.

The National Party came to power in 1948 in a surprise election victory. There were many reasons why they triumphed, but none more so than because they offered segregation of the races in simple, easy-to-grasp terms. To give effect to this philosophy, the South African Bureau for Racial Affairs (SABRA) was launched. This led directly to a number of racial laws, including the Population Registration Act, which assigned every person to a racial category, and the Group Areas Act, which enforced separate urban areas for each race group.

The myriad other repressive measures, which led to growing

resistance and brought even greater oppression and a reign of terror by the security establishment, are impressively documented by the museum. Set in seven hectares of superbly landscaped grounds, it has 22 exhibition areas designed by a team of curators, filmmakers and historians. Film-footage, text panels and artefacts are arranged in such a way as to recreate the experience of life under apartheid.

The Freedom Park

Pretoria's ambitious The Freedom Park, which pays tribute to those who fell during South Africa's turbulent history, is showing signs that it will become one of the country's premier heritage sites.

Best of the Struggle for Freedom sites

- Red Location Museum (Port Elizabeth) – like the Hector Peterson and Apartheid museums, this is an architectural gem that brings history to life
- Robben Island (if the ferry is running) – a celebration of the spirit of heroes
- Constitution Hill (Johannesburg) – a living museum that embodies the best of what people fought for
- Hector Peterson Museum (Soweto) – a living memorial that is a fitting tribute to this important event
- The Freedom Park (Pretoria) – a peaceful, contemplative place lacking all the triumphalism of the Voortrekker Monument, which it looks on to
- Apartheid Museum (Johannesburg) – if you can get past the fact that this was funded by people who

made their fortunes selling skin lightening creams to turn black women white during apartheid

Avoid like the plague . . .

- Burning Truth (Fordsburg) – there are more attractive rubbish bins in Johannesburg
- Nobel Square – there is something deeply disturbing when shopping centres like the V&A exploit icons for commercial gain. Ditto Sandton Square with its amazingly awful statue of Nelson Mandela

BATTLEFIELDS AND HERITAGE SITES

Pre-1994 South African history is a litany of conflicts and rivalries between the many groups that lived or had interests in the region. The most important South African battlefields, however, are from after the Dutch settlers arrived in 1652 to the end of the Anglo-Boer War in 1902.

While the Dutch traded with the local inhabitants, there were also serious disputes, which led to three Khoikhoi-Dutch Wars around Cape Town between 1659 and 1677. The settlers' biggest problem, though, was protecting their sea route to the East. This they were able to do until 1795, when Britain first took occupation of the Cape after the Battle of Muizenberg. The British handed back the Cape to the Dutch, but retook it in 1806 at the Battle of Blaauwberg. These, however, were minor in comparison to what was to come as the settlers expanded eastwards.

In the Eastern Cape there were nine Frontier Wars between 1779 and 1879, in which the Xhosa lost most of their lands. At about the same time as the first of these, Zulu king Shaka was waging the Ndwandwe-Zulu War in which he prevailed at Gqoki Hill and Mhlatuze River.

When the Boers arrived in the province they defeated Shaka's successor, Dingaan, at the Battle of Blood River on 16 December 1838. But soon they migrated inland after the arrival of the British. The British fought the Zulu in the Anglo-Zulu War of 1879 with the most notable encounters at Isandlwana and Rorke's Drift. They then turned their attention to the Boers of the Transvaal in the first Anglo-Boer War, but withdrew after the setback at Majuba Hill in 1881. And the second Anglo-Boer War of 1899-1902 would add many more battlefields.

Did you know?

Guerrilla warfare was first used in South Africa by the Boers, as were concentration camps, invented by the British.

Anglo-Zulu War

There are numerous Anglo-Zulu War battlefields in northern KwaZulu-Natal. This is as a result of British forces invading Zululand to subjugate the Zulu under Cetshwayo.

The spark for war was provided by border incidents, especially along a disputed strip of land on the Zululand border with Natal running from Rorke's Drift to the Pongola River. An ultimatum was delivered to Cetshwayo on 11 December 1878, which would expire on 11 January the following year. Cetshwayo did not respond and Lord Chelmsford invaded Zululand in January 1879 without waiting for British authority to do so. He had three columns, their objective the royal capital at Ulundi, which entered Zululand unopposed at Lower Tugela, Utrecht and Rorke's Drift.

Did you know?

The Anglo-Zulu War was waged illegally, as permission had not been granted to Chelmsford by Britain.

Part of Chelmsford's column advancing from Rorke's Drift encamped at Isandlwana under Lieutenant Colonel Henry Pulleine, while Chelmsford moved on to join a reconnoitring party. Largely unprepared, the camp was surprised by 20 000 Zulu in what was to be their most decisive victory. A 4 000-strong Zulu reserve group moved on from here to Rorke's Drift, but were repulsed after 10 hours of fierce battle. While the Zulu besieged Eshowe and won further battles at Hlobane and Intombi Spruit, they were eventually defeated at the Battle of Ulundi on 4 July 1880.

Did you know?

Isandlwana is the worst defeat the British have ever suffered against an indigenous army. However, they redeemed themselves at Rorke's Drift, where more Victoria Crosses were awarded than on any other day of battle in British history.

The First Anglo-Boer War (1880-1881)

Majuba Hill near Volksrust is the site of one of the greatest blunders in British military history.

In 1877 Britain annexed the Transvaal Republic, which led to the start of the first Anglo-Boer War (known by the Boers as the War of Independence) on 16 December 1880. After a number of battles the combatants met at Majuba Hill on 27 February 1881. The British commander, Major-General Sir George Colley, had the previous day occupied the summit of the hill, presumably to outflank the Boer positions at Laing's Nek. Nearly half his men were from the 92nd (Gordon) Highlanders.

Colley, who until then was highly regarded, took no artillery with him nor did he ask his troops to dig in. While he assumed the Boers would disperse when they became aware of his position, made abundantly clear by Highlanders shouting and waving their fists, they instead organised a storming party led by Nicolas Smit. Smit, for the first time in warfare, employed the fire-and-movement tactic to keep the British at bay while his three attack groups got into position. Just after midnight they reached the summit and engaged the enemy with tremendous fire while avoiding hand-to-hand combat.

In panic, the surviving British fell into disarray and fled down the hill, where many more were killed, injured or captured. They tried to mount a rearguard action, but this had little impact. Britain lost 92 men, including Colley, while the Boers lost only one. This ignominious defeat led to the British signing a truce on 6 March and a peace treaty two weeks later.

Today, the summit provides wonderful vistas over northern KwaZulu-Natal. From the south summit you can see Ingogo where the film *Zulu* was shot. To the east is Charlestown, where Mahatma Gandhi was forced from the train because of the colour of his skin.

Did you know?

Lieutenant Hector Macdonald was freed after capture by the Boers because of his bravery.

The Second Anglo-Boer War (1899–1902)

One of the most bitter conflicts of pre-apartheid South African history was that between Boer and Briton, which spiralled into the Anglo-Boer War of 1899-1902, sometimes known as the Second Anglo-Boer War. There are many well-maintained battlefields from the first phase of the war, especially those around the siege towns of Kimberley and Ladysmith.

The war began on 11 October 1899, when the Boers took the offensive on four fronts: north into then Southern Rhodesia; west into the Northern Cape; south into the northeastern Cape; and east into Natal, where they fought their first battle at Talana Hill at Dundee on 20 October. The following day the Boers suffered their first defeat at Elandslaagte in Natal.

In the first five months of the war, however, that setback was a rarity. They besieged Mafikeng and Kimberley on 14 October and Ladysmith two weeks later and, in the field, inflicted a series of embarrassments on the British that culminated in the calamitous disasters at Stormberg (10 December), Magersfontein (11 December) and Colenso (15 December) that came to be known in Britain as 'black week'.

In desperation Britain sent her two top soldiers, Lord 'Bobs' Roberts and his Chief of Staff, Lord Kitchener, to halt the devastation. No sooner had they arrived than General Louis Botha captured Spioenkop in Natal on 24 January 1900. The tide, however, turned in favour of the British as their forces reached full strength. On 15 February Kimberley was relieved, on the 27th General Cronje surrendered at Paardeberg and on 1 March Ladysmith was relieved. Soon after the relief of Mafikeng on 17 May, the Orange Free State then the Transvaal were annexed to the Crown.

All the siege towns have monuments and museums dedicated to the Anglo-Boer War, with well-organised tours of the battlefields.

Especially impressive is Magersfontein, which has an interactive
centre, lookout points and a restaurant.

Did you know?

The first shot of the Anglo-Boer War was fired by Boer gunner Jaap van Deventer at Kraaipan between Kimberley and Mafikeng. Ironically, he was knighted after the war for services to the British Empire.

The Struggle for Freedom

The Freedom Struggle is a fascinating and enduring aspect of our history, with Struggle heritage sites all over the country.

The struggle began when the Khoikhoi resisted the establishment of a refreshment station at Table Bay by the Dutch East India Company on 6 April 1652. But until January 1912, when the forerunner to the ANC was established, the battle against growing oppression was localised. And even then it would remain fairly passive until the advent of apartheid in 1948, which ushered in a period of repression infinitely worse than anything experienced before.

At the behest of young activists like Nelson Mandela, the ANC began to change its direction to a mass-based movement intent on liberation from apartheid. Growing resistance culminated in the Sharpeville Massacre in March 1960, in which 69 protestors were killed by police. In panic the government declared a state of emergency and banned the ANC and other smaller liberation movements.

The ANC responded by taking the struggle underground and establishing an armed wing, Umkhonto we Sizwe (Spear of the Nation). The government, in turn, tightened its repressive measures and crushed the movement, forcing those leaders who were not incarcerated on Robben Island to flee overseas. After regrouping, the ANC in exile and internal underground structures were able to bring such pressure to bear on the apartheid government that it unbanned all liberation movements in 1990, freed imprisoned leaders and entered negotiations, which culminated in the first democratic elections being held on 27 April 1994.

Did you know?

Nelson Mandela was known as the Black Pimpernel during the early years of the Freedom Struggle.

Natural

ATTRACTIONS

South Africa has eight World Heritage Sites.

Cradle of Humankind

The Cradle of Humankind in the beautiful Sterkfontein Valley near Johannesburg was proclaimed a World Heritage Site on 2 December 1999. It was approved by UNESCO on the basis that: 'The area contains an exceptionally large and scientifically significant group of sites, which throw light on the earliest ancestors of humankind. They constitute a vast reserve of scientific information, the potential of which is enormous.'

It comprises a unique band of palaeo-anthropological sites across 47 000 hectares in the north-western corner of Gauteng and parts of North West Province. It has yielded some of the most extensive fossil and artefact finds on earth, particularly for the period between four and one million years ago, leading scientists to believe that the human family tree took root here. Over time these first people used their freed hands to shape the first tool, which would herald global technology, spoke the first word and slowly migrated on a journey to populate the earth.

There are 13 explored sites within the Cradle of Humankind, with many more still to be discovered. Among these are the Sterkfontein Caves, where the famous Mrs Ples and Little Foot fossils were found; Kromdraai, which contains later hominid specimens; Gondolin, which is home to an astonishing 90 000 fossil specimens; and Swartkrans, where burnt bones point to the earliest controlled use of fire at least a million years ago.

Vredefort Dome

The Vredefort Dome is an enormous, two-billion-year-old meteorite impact crater near the Free State town of Parys. Bigger than Table Mountain, it is the oldest and largest impact site in the world. Visitors can take part in Dome trails, which include full-day and overnight hikes, and there is also a canoe trail and a mountain-bike trail.

Mapungubwe Cultural Landscape

Where the Shashe and Limpopo rivers meet, bringing three countries together – South Africa, Zimbabwe and Botswana – are the remains of an Iron Age kingdom. In 1932 a hunting party found evidence of this past civilisation – pottery, iron tools, fragments of jewellery – on Mapungubwe Hill. The discovery was brought to the attention of the University of Pretoria, and an archaeological exploration began, which revealed the existence of a highly developed kingdom some 700 to 1 000 years ago.

Trade beads originating from India, Egypt and the Arab world, as well as evidence of contact with Asia, have turned the theory that Europeans were first to bring international trade to southern Africa on its head. It is also believed the inhabitants of the settlement kept cattle, sheep and goats and cultivated millet and sorghum. A hierarchy is reflected in the layout of the settlement, with royalty housed on Mapungubwe Hill and their subjects below. A small golden rhinoceros, made of wood and covered in gold foil, is the most famous artefact uncovered and has become a symbol of the site; it is housed at the Mapungubwe Museum at Pretoria University. Today the hill, along with another excavation site known as K2, form part of the Mapungubwe National Park.

Cape Floral Kingdom

The Cape of Good Hope falls into the Cape Floral Kingdom, which contains an astonishing 20 per cent of all the floral species of Africa, most endemic to South Africa. Many of these plants are part of the fynbos group, which includes proteas, ericas and restios.

The Table Mountain National Park, which stretches from Cape Point to Signal Hill across a range of mountains, falls within this and includes a combination of mountains, ocean, beaches and forests. Also here on the slopes of Table Mountain is the Kirstenbosch National Botanical Garden, which is one of Cape Town's top attractions. Situated on Rhodes Drive in Newlands, it is renowned for its indigenous plants and fantastic theme gardens. Covering 528 hectares, it is also popular for its summer concerts.

Did you know?

The Cape Floral Kingdom, the smallest in the world but with the most variety, has more plant species than either New Zealand or the British Isles.

Robben Island

Declared a World Heritage Site in 1999, it is where Nelson Mandela and other anti-apartheid activists were incarcerated.

This bean-shaped island, the largest in the country, is situated in Table Bay with superb views of Cape Town nine kilometres away. Its high point is only 30 metres above sea level at Minto Hill, atop which is the oldest lighthouse in the southern hemisphere. The first recorded landing on Robben Island was in 1498, when Vasco da Gama's support fleet took temporary refuge in its waters. Its situation also made it ideal as a place of quarantine and during much of the later British occupation it was used as a leper colony.

But it is as a place of banishment and exile that it is notorious. Miscreant sailors were offloaded here, as were Muslim activists fighting Dutch colonisation in the Far East. The British, after taking permanent occupation at the beginning of the nineteenth century, continued this tradition by banishing troublesome traditional leaders who were opposing settler incursion into the interior.

In 1960 the government used a section of the newly constructed maximum security section as a political prison, which is now the museum. The inmates were subject to hard labour and brutality, but few were broken and the epic of their experience is today symbolic of the triumph of ordinary people over an extraordinary crime against humanity.

Did you know?

Robben Island and Table Mountain are the only two World Heritage Sites visible from each other.

uKhahlamba Drakensberg World Heritage Site

The dominant feature of KwaZulu-Natal is the Drakensberg Mountains, which range from the Eastern Cape to Mpumalanga. They were created millions of years ago when an ancient seabed reared up to form a great escarpment that was then sculpted by erosion. It is a scenic wonder most awesome in the Champagne Valley of the Central Drakensberg, which was proclaimed a World Heritage Site in November 2000.

This is a region that has moved and inspired through the ages. Bushmen decorated it with some of the finest rock art ever seen, it inspired JRR Tolkien's Middle Earth in *The Lord of the Rings* and galvanised the Tungay family to found the internationally renowned Drakensberg Boys' Choir School in 1967. It is not difficult to see why. At the heart of its attraction is an Eden of gentle rolling hills and vertical-faced mountains, of domes and cowls and spearlike pinnacles, of endless valleys and plunging waterfalls, of giant yellowwoods and dazzling snow.

Did you know?

The Thukela Falls in the
Drakensberg are the second
highest in the world.

iSimangaliso Wetland Park

The jewel in the crown of Zululand in KwaZulu-Natal is undoubtedly the iSimangaliso Wetland Park.

Few places in the world rival the magnificence of iSimangaliso on the Elephant Coast. Its Zulu name tells you that 'you are in the land of miracles'. It is said that when Shaka died, Ujeqe, his aide given to keeping all his secrets, fled as it was customary for this person to be buried with his monarch. He wandered into Thongaland (present-day Maputaland) and on his return exclaimed, 'I saw wonders and miracles in the flat land and lakes of Thonga.'

iSimangaliso was listed as South Africa's first World Heritage Site in 1999. It covers approximately 300 000 hectares, including 220 kilometres of pristine Indian Ocean coastline and contains the largest protected wetland in South Africa. It extends from the north in Kosi Bay, where ancient fishing communities thrived, to the village of St Lucia in the south. The park is a robust interaction of eight interlinking ecosystems, which are home to a profusion of fish species and fauna and flora. Then there are the 25 000-year-old coastal dunes, which are amongst the highest in the world. They have been linked to old agricultural practices, trading routes and Zulu explorations.

Richtersveld Cultural and Botanical Landscape

Mountain range upon mountain range – there is no limit to the view. The Ai-Ais/Richtersveld National Park and World Heritage Site, which protects South Africa's only mountain desert, presents a striking display of canyons, reefs, escarpments, pinnacles, mazes and lakes of stone. Great edifices of jagged black rock, weathered and carved, float on shimmering heat waves. This is Die Verdwaalwêreld – The World of Disappearing – the land God created in anger.

Life appears improbable here, yet myriad species use remarkable survival tactics to defy a land of extremes. The richest variety of succulents on the planet, most endemic, are found here, nourished by the !Gariep River (the Nama name for the Orange River), a few millimetres of rain a year and fog from the nearby Atlantic Ocean that washes over the mountains through winter. The region was earmarked as a national park in 1972, principally to protect this unique flora. Despite the stark landscape, research has shown that people have lived in the Richtersveld for at least 3 000 years.

UNESCO BIOSPHERE RESERVES

South Africa has six UNESCO Biosphere Reserves, which promote a balanced relationship between man and sensitive environments that contain a mosaic of ecological systems.

Kogelberg

This was South Africa's first UNESCO Biosphere Reserve and incorporates marine, coastal mountain ranges and parts of the Cape Floristic Kingdom of the Western Cape.

Cape West Coast

It includes marine, beach, frontal dune systems, pans, wetlands, part of the Cape Floristic Kingdom and rocky outcrops of the West Coast north of Cape Town.

Cape Winelands

Stretching from Kogelberg, this biosphere reserve focuses on the Cape Fold Belt Mountain Range and includes key aspects of the Cape Floristic Kingdom.

Kruger to Canyons

This is a massive biosphere reserve that includes most of the Kruger National Park and the Blyde River Canyon. Three biomes (grasslands, savannah and forest) are found within it.

Did you know?

The Blyde River Canyon is the largest green canyon in the world, and the third biggest overall.

Waterberg

The water reservoir for the bushveld area of Limpopo Province, this biosphere reserve contains important Bushman rock art sites and game reserves.

Vhembe

South Africa's latest biosphere reserve, it includes parts of the northern Kruger National Park, Makuleke Wetlands, Soutpansberg range, Mapungubwe, Blouberg and the Makgabeng Plateau, which is noted for Bushman rock art.

SOUTH AFRICAN BIOMES

Fynbos

This biome is otherwise known as the Cape Floral Kingdom, which is a World Heritage Site. (See p 113.)

Grasslands

The South African grasslands biome, lying between 25° and 31° longitude and 25° and 33° latitude, covers a third of the country (339 237 square kilometres) across seven provinces. It reaches from the interior of the Eastern Cape and KwaZulu-Natal, over the escarpment and into the central plateau.

Did you know?

The term 'grassland' implies that the biome consists only of grass species. In fact, only one in six plant species in the biome is a grass. The remainder are bulbous plants such as arum lilies, orchids, red-hot pokers, aloes, watsonias, gladioli and ground orchids.

The grasslands biome is under the most developmental pressure, mostly unsustainable, as the majority of the population resides here. It is at the heart of economic, agricultural and industrial activity, with Gauteng as the country's economic powerhouse. Key impacts on its biodiversity include urban development; agriculture and game farming, which also operates in the tourism sector; plantation forestry; and mining, especially for coal.

Did you know?

Three World Heritage Sites are found in the South African grasslands biome – the Cradle of Humankind, uKhahlamba Drakensberg Park and the Vredefort Dome.

Did you know?

The South African grasslands biome harbours an exceptionally rich indigenous floristic diversity, second only to the Cape Floral Kingdom.

Savannah

The savannah biome, characterised by grassy shrubland, covers 46 per cent of the country in an arc from the Lowveld to the Kalahari. It is the largest biome in South Africa and home to some of its premier national parks, including the Kruger, Mapungubwe and Kgalagadi. As the plants here are grazed by antelope, it is the perfect environment for predators higher up the food chain, which is why most of the game reserves are found here.

Forest

The smallest of South Africa's biomes, covering about 0,25 per cent of the land surface, it is contained in small, high rainfall pockets from the Garden Route of the southern Cape coast and along the eastern seaboard and into the Eastern Escarpment. However, some of South Africa's most magnificent scenery is here: the lake system at Wilderness, the steaming forests of the Tsitsikamma and the misty mountains of Magoebaskloof.

Succulent Karoo

Found along the western seaboard beyond the Cape Fold Mountains, this biome is characterised by low winter rainfall and dry, scorching summers. There are few grasses here and the plant types are predominantly vygies and stonecrops. For its size, it contains the most plant species in the world, mainly succulents.

The region, especially Namaqualand, is noted for mass spring bloomings, mainly where the land is degraded or fallow. It is a place of rare and exquisite beauty when it hosts one of nature's most extravagant spectacles that cloaks it in a riotous tapestry of billions of blooming annuals, herbs, succulents and bulbs. 'Field after field of cleared plateau and mountain slopes were ablaze with gorgeous colour, being absolutely covered with the most brilliant-hued flowers,' enthused Fred Cornell in 1913 in his diary as he witnessed the scene from a train window on one of his prospecting expeditions to the area. 'Here morgen after morgen of glorious crimson; there, half a mountainside of mustard yellow, in startling contrast to the other half of azure blue.'

Nama Karoo

The Nama Karoo biome covers the Great Karoo of the central plateau and stretches from the Northern Cape and into parts of the Western Cape, Free State and Eastern Cape. The vegetation is clumpy grass and dwarf shrubland.

Desert

While most of the true desert in southern Africa is found in Namibia, there is a small portion in South Africa, mainly around the Springbokvlakte area of the Richtersveld. This is a much harsher climate than either the Succulent or Nama Karoo, and vegetation is mainly perennial grasses. The area is a haven for insects, especially beetles.

Did you know?

The world's smallest succulent plants are found in South Africa.

All parks in KwaZulu-Natal fall under Ezemvelo KZN Parks, which is why there are no national parks in the province. They have always believed they can do a better job, which in many cases they do.

Addo Elephant National Park

Proclaimed in 1931 to save the elephants of the Eastern Cape, which then numbered only seven, the Addo Elephant Park is today a Big Seven mega-park that has the densest population of elephants on earth and includes a 120 000 hectare marine reserve that incorporates islands that are home to breeding colonies of Cape gannets and African penguins. These waters offer fine viewing for southern right whales and great white sharks. Within the park is the largest dune field in the southern hemisphere. If you like small things, the flightless dung beetle is endemic to Addo.

Did you know?

Bird Island in the Addo Elephant National Park has the largest breeding colony of Cape gannets in the world and the second largest of African penguins.

Agulhas National Park

Agulhas, which is included in the Agulhas National Park, is the southernmost tip of Africa (and not Cape Point as many think). The lighthouse, which incorporates a museum, is of special interest. But it was not enough to save the *Zoetendal*, *HMS Birkenhead* and *HMS Arniston* which were wrecked along this treacherous strip of the Cape of Storms.

Did you know?

It is myth that the *HMS Birkenhead* established the seafaring practice of 'women and children first'. This honour, in fact, goes to the *Abercrombie Robinson*, which sank in Table Bay in the Western Cape a decade earlier, in 1842.

Augrabies Falls National Park

This park encompasses the 56-metre Augrabies Falls on the !Gariep (Orange) River. It takes its name from the Khoi word 'Aukoerebis', meaning Place of Great Noise.

Did you know?

The !Gariep River (Nama name for Orange River) is the longest river in South Africa.

Established on the Breede River near Swellendam in the Western Cape to save the highly endangered Bontebok. Once numbering only 17, there are now more than 3 000.

Camdeboo National Park

The Camdeboo National Park encompasses Graaff-Reinet in the Eastern Cape. Its main feature is the Valley of Desolation, with its spectacular dolerite pillars.

Garden Route National Park

The Garden Route National Park along the Cape South Coast came about with the amalgamation in 2009 of the Wilderness National Park, Knysna National Lake Area and Tsitsikamma National Park. The Wilderness section of the park is defined by its lake system, relic forests in the Touws River Gorge and ancient dunes. The sandbanks and salt marshes of the Knysna Lake, dominated by the imposing Knysna Heads, teem with life, including the endangered Knysna seahorse. The incredibly scenic Tsitsikamma portion protects the indigenous forests and marine environment.

Did you know?

The Tsitsikamma National Park (now incorporated into the Garden Route National Park) was South Africa's first marine reserve.

Golden Gate Highlands National Park

This beautiful eastern Free State mountain park takes its name from the play of sunlight on sandstone cliffs. Of special interest here are the rare bearded vulture (lammergeier) and bald ibis.

Greater Mapungubwe Transfrontier Park

See Mapungubwe Cultural Landscape under World Heritage Sites, p 112.

Karoo National Park

Near Beaufort West in the Western Cape, the Karoo National Park protects a sample of the largest ecosystem in South Africa. It has one of the highest concentrations of black eagle breeding pairs in Africa.

Kgalagadi Transfrontier Park

This is an amalgamation of the Kalahari Gemsbok National Park in South Africa and the Gemsbok National Park in Botswana. It is noted for its fossil dune system, black-maned lions and graceful gemsbok.

The gemsbok is superbly adapted to life in a desert because of a feature it has evolved to raise its body temperature for up to eight hours to a level normally considered lethal. It does not sweat to cool down; rather, in conditions of extreme heat, it allows its body temperature to soar to 45 °C without ill effect. Not only does this conserve water, but it allows heat to flow from it. This feat is made possible by a fine network of blood vessels – called the carotid rete – located immediately below the brain.

Kruger National Park

A proclamation was issued by President Kruger establishing the Sabie Game Reserve, later to become the Kruger National Park, on 26 March 1898. Little more was done before the Anglo-Boer War a year later. The first tourists, who were allowed to carry firearms and sleep in the bush, entered the reserve in 1927.

The Kruger National Park is the jewel in the crown of South African National Parks, containing one of the greatest assemblages of life on earth. While most equate it with the Big Five – lion, leopard, elephant, rhino and buffalo – or the 507 species of birds, it is also home to another 142 mammal species, 118 species of reptile, 33 species of amphibian, 49 species of fish, 336 species of trees, in excess of 1 600 species of shrub, grasses, ferns, woody lianas, aloes and herbs, and 700 species of invertebrates, excluding insects, of which there are 227 species of butterfly alone.

Did you know?

The Kruger National Park was not conceived in the late nineteenth century to protect wilderness, as myth has it, but as a nursery for game preservation to ensure continued supply for hunters.

Marakele National Park

One of the newer national parks, it is set in the Waterberg Mountains of Limpopo Province. It is another of the Big Five reserves.

Mokala National Park

South Africa's newest national park, south-west of Kimberley in the Northern Cape. Its main feature is the camelthorn trees found in drier areas.

Mountain Zebra National Park

Proclaimed in 1937, this Eastern Cape national park saved the mountain zebra from extinction.

Namaqua National Park

Namaqualand is a place of rare and exquisite beauty that each spring hosts one of nature's most extravagant spectacles when it is cloaked in a riotous tapestry of billions of blooming annuals, herbs, succulents and bulbs. The nucleus of this Northern Cape park, proclaimed in 1999, is the well-known and enlarged Skilpad Wildflower Reserve near Kamieskroon in the Kamiesberge and the area between the Groen and Spoeg rivers, which will allow for the protection of marine ecosystems as well as the associated estuaries.

Did you know?

There are an estimated 3 500 species of plants in Namaqualand, with more than 1 000 endemic to the region.

Table Mountain National Park

See World Heritage Sites, p 113.

Tankwa Karoo National Park

Taking in the Roggeveld Mountains and the Cederberg, this national park an hour from Cape Town contains stunning landscapes and conserves a section of the Succulent Karoo biome.

West Coast National Park

The focus of this national park is the Langebaan Lagoon on the West Coast. It includes the Postberg Flower Reserve and a number of islands that are a roost for seabirds.

Ai-Ais/Richtersveld Transfrontier Park

See World Heritage Sites, p 117.

Best of the Parks

- Garden Route National Park – for its spectacular beauty
- iSimangaliso Wetland Park – paradise
- uKhahlamba Drakensberg World Heritage Site – awe-inspiring and accessible
- Mapungubwe National Park – fascinating, spectacular setting, with the best accommodation options of any national park
- Table Mountain National Park – iconic
- Kruger National Park – big enough to preserve a slice of Africa that has been largely lost
- Kgalagadi Transfrontier Park – a place that lets the imagination run riot
- Hluhluwe-Imfolozi Game Reserve – does everything a park should
- Ai-Ais/Richtersveld Transfrontier Park – like arriving on the set of an other-wordly science fiction production

Disappointing

- Augrabies Falls National Park – bit like a prostate-strangled urinary tract trickle since some fool built two dams upriver
- Namaqua National Park – except in flower season during spring

Don't bother with . . .

- Bontebok National Park – unless you really, really like bontebok
- Skukuza in the Kruger National Park – unless you really, really like tour buses belching diesel fumes
- The town of St Lucia in iSimangaliso – unless you really, really like drunken throwbacks in two-tone shirts

Hluhluwe-Imfolozi Game Reserve

Once the hunting ground of Zulu kings, this Zululand park is renowned for its efforts to conserve the white rhino. This is Big Five and birdwatching territory, with over 300 bird species.

Did you know?

Hluhluwe-Imfolozi Game Reserve, proclaimed in 1895, is the oldest conservancy in Africa.

iSimangaliso Wetland Park

See World Heritage Sites, p 116.

Ithala Game Reserve

The main features of this park in northern KwaZulu-Natal are its Greenstone Belt rocks and beautiful setting in the Ngotshe Mountains overlooking the Phongolo River.

Mkhuze Game Reserve

To the north-west of iSimangaliso, Mkhuze is one of South Africa's premier birdwatching destinations with over 420 species. Among the birds found here are the pinkbacked and white pelicans.

uKhahlamba Drakensberg World Heritage Site

See World Heritage Sites, p 115.

Future National Parks

South African National Parks is planning a marine reserve at Pondoland and a grasslands park, currently the only biome in South Africa not represented by a national park.

Best photogenic hot spots

• God's Window, Mpumalanga

- Namaqualand in springtime
- Top of Table Mountain
- Augrabies Falls
- Blyde River Canyon
- The Drakensberg
- Bloubergstrand
- Golden Gate National Park
- Long Street, Cape Town in the wee hours of the morning where you will see wild animals of a different kind

MAMMALS

The Big Six

Elephant
Lion
Rhino
Leopard
Buffalo
Southern right whales

Endemic mammals

Blesbok
Bontebok
Black wildebeest
Cape mountain zebra
Grey rhebok
Riverine rabbit

Extinct mammals

The last blue buck was shot in 1799 in what is now the Western Cape. This antelope became the first southern African extinction, followed by the quagga (something lik a half horse, half zebra) in 1883.

Endangered mammals

Black rhino
Riverine rabbit
African wild dog

Threatened mammals

Brown hyena
Honeybadger
Serval cat

Vulnerable mammals

Cheetah
Roan antelope
Sable antelope

Top animal and bird sanctuaries

- De Wildt Cheetah and Wildlife Trust – based in the North West province, this sanctuary is aimed at protecting, conserving and breeding cheetah

- SanWild Wildlife Rehabilitation Centre and Sanctuary – situated in the Limpopo province, this is one of South Africa's finest wildlife sanctuaries, dedicated to the rehabilitation of wild animals
- Moholoholo Rehabilitation Centre – located at the base of the Drakensberg, this establishment is dedicated to rescuing and saving injured or orphaned wild animals
- Monkeyland Primate Sanctuary – this sanctuary in Plettenberg Bay caters for several types of primates. Notably, the animals are not in cages but are free to move about the forests
- Enkosini, Mpumalanga – this wildlife sanctuary was formed to protect and preserve Africa's wild animals and their habitat. The focus is on the African lion and other wild predators
- Centre for Animal Rehabilitation and Education (CARE) – established in 1987 by Rito Miljo, this was the very first animal rehabilitation centre in Limpopo. Today CARE is home to 280 baboons, as well as other wild creatures
- The Barberspan Bird Sanctuary – this bird sanctuary in the North West province is one of the largest waterfowl sanctuaries in South Africa.
- Elephant Sanctuary – there are two elephant sanctuaries in South Africa, one at Hartbeespoort Dam and the other in Plettenberg Bay. Enjoy up-close-and-personal experiences with these large animals. The focus is on education
- Hout Bay World of Birds – a notable bird sanctuary
- Solole Private Game Reserve – Western Cape, dedicated to breeding the Cape Buffalo

Ramsar Sites, taking their name from the Iranian city where the Convention on Wetlands was signed in 1971, are wetlands of international importance. All of these are noted for their richness in bird species, among others. There are 17 Ramsar Sites in South Africa.

Western Cape

Verlorenvlei
Langebaan
De Mond State Forest
De Hoop Vlei
Wilderness Lakes

Northern Cape

Orange River Mouth Wetland

Did you know?

The kori bustard, found in South Africa, is the world's largest flying bird.

North West

Barberspan

Nylsvley Nature Reserve

Gauteng

Blesbok Spruit

Free State

Seekoeivlei

KwaZulu-Natal

Natal Drakensberg Park
Ndumo Game Reserve
Khosi Bay System
Lake Sibaya
St Lucia System
Turtle Beaches and Coral Reefs of Tongaland

Mpumalanga

Verloren Vallei Nature Reserve

Worth a mention

- While still being evaluated for Ramsar status, the wetlands of Wakkerstroom on the Mpumalanga highlands are an absolute gem

Top birding spots

- Nylsvley – this important birding site covers some 4 000 hectares across the Nyl floodplain in Limpopo Province and is one of South Africa's most prolific birding sites
- The Geelbek Hide at Langebaan (West Coast National Park) – one of the best wetland hides in southern Africa according to *Getaway* magazine, the local outdoor-lover's bible
- Mkhuze Game Reserve – Over 450 species are found in the Mkhuze Game Reserve in KwaZulu-Natal; ask one of the qualified guides to show you the ropes
- Marievale Bird Sanctuary – you'll find this excellent wetlands sanctuary on the outskirts of Johannesburg
- Wakkerstroom, Mpumalanga – a favourite birding spot in South Africa. Many of South Africa's endemic bird species can be seen here
- Kgalagadi Transfrontier Park – if raptors are your thing, then Kgalagadi is the place to be – over 40 species of raptors have been identified in this region
- Ndumo Reserve – this reserve in northern KwaZulu-Natal is known by inner-circle birders as a fantastic spot and there are over 400 species to look out for
- Zululand Birding Route – visit the abundant Ongoye Forest in KwaZulu-Natal, which forms part of the Zululand Birding Route
- Magoebaskloof – Rooikoppies, The Woodbush Reserve and the Debengeni Falls are good places to spot the rare Cape Parrot
- Addo Elephant Park – this national park boasts over 270 species and is definitely a worthwhile birding spot

There are nine South African national botanical gardens, situated in five of its biomes.

- Free State National Botanical Garden in Bloemfontein
- Hantam National Botanical Garden near Niewoudtville in the Northern Cape
- Harold Porter National Botanical Garden at Betty's Bay in the Western Cape
- Karoo Desert National Botanical Garden near Worcester in the Western Cape
- Kirstenbosch National Botanical Garden in Cape Town
- KwaZulu-Natal National Botanical Garden in Pietermaritzburg
- Lowveld National Botanical Garden in Nelspruit, Mpumalanga
- Pretoria National Botanical Garden
- Walter Sisulu National Botanical Garden in Johannesburg

Did you know?

There are 6 million planted trees in Johannesburg, making it the world's largest man-made forest.

Did you know?

Limpopo is home to the Rain Queen, who presides over the Modjadji Cycad Reserve that contains some of the oldest cycad specimens on earth.

BLUE FLAG BEACHES

South Africa is blessed with a long coastline and fantastic beaches. Some of the most beautiful are Victoria Bay and Tsitsikamma along the Garden Route and those of Tongaland in northern KwaZulu-Natal. Blue Flag status is an international certification for safety, cleanliness, amenities and environmental standards, of which the country has 29.

Eastern Cape

- Boknes Beach, near Port Alfred
- Dolphin Beach, Jeffrey's Bay
- Gonubie Beach, East London
- Hobie Beach, Port Elizabeth
- Humewood Beach, Port Elizabeth
- Kariega Beach, Kenton-on-Sea
- Kelly's Beach, Port Alfred
- Robberg 5 Beach, Plettenberg Bay
- Wells Estate, north of Port Elizabeth

KwaZulu-Natal

- Alkantstrand Beach, Richards Bay
- Margate Beach, South Coast
- Marina/San Lameer Beach, South Coast
- Ramsgate Beach, South Coast
- Trafalgar Beach, South Coast

Northern Cape

- McDougalls Bay Beach, Port Nolloth

- Big Bay, Bloubergstrand Beach, Cape Town
- Bikini Beach, Gordon's Bay
- Camps Bay Beach, Cape Town
- Clifton 4th Beach, Cape Town
- Grotto Beach, Hermanus
- Hartenbos Beach, Mossel Bay
- Hawston Beach, near Hermanus
- Kleinmond Beach, near Hermanus
- Lappiesbaai Beach, Stilbaai
- Mnandi Beach, Cape Town
- Muizenberg Beach, Cape Town
- Santos Beach, Mossel Bay
- Strandfontein Beach, Cape Town
- Yzerfontein Beach, West Coast

Best beaches in South Africa

- Turtle Beach – in Tongaland in northern KwaZulu-Natal; this is a long, lonely stretch of pristine beach
- Victoria Bay – near George along the Garden Route; it is accessed by a steep, winding road. Great views, great surfing, great for whale watching
- Tsitsikamma Beach – along the Garden Route; arguably the most beautiful setting in the country, framed by verdant cliffs and pounded by mighty waves
- Wilderness Beach – along the Garden Route; it is a great place to unwind after enjoying one of the great walking or canoeing trails in the area
- King's Beach – in Port Elizabeth; where King George dipped his toes in 1947, it is often rated the best

beach in the country
- Boulders Beach – in Simon's Town; for the penguins and great setting
- Camps Bay Beach – in Cape Town; spectacular backdrop
- Clifton 4th Beach – in Cape Town; the place to be seen
- Blroubergstrand – in Cape Town; for the best views of Table Mountain
- Strand – in the Western Cape; one of the best, safest swimming beaches around. A gem for those who love beach walks

Disappointing

- The beaches of East London and many on the KwaZulu-Natal South Coast

Best avoided

- Durban beaches, many of which were recently stripped of their Blue Flag status, unless of course you dream of being crammed with unruly mobs in a sea of effluent

OUTDOOR ACTIVITIES AND ADVENTURES

Best OhmiGod adventure experiences

- Diving with tiger sharks in KwaZulu-Natal
- Bloukrans Bungee on the Garden Route
- Cage diving with great white sharks in the Western Cape

- Kloofing Suicide Gorge
- Surfing Dungeons in Hout Bay
- Climbing a frozen waterfall in the Drakensberg
- Diving Wondergat in the North West

Don't bother with ...

- Crocodile cage diving in the Little Karoo. The old croc is so slow and clumsy you may well fall asleep underwater

Did you know?

More than half of the world's paragliding records have been set in South Africa.

Best civilised adventures

- Game viewing on horseback in the Free State
- Hot-air ballooning over the Magaliesberg
- Taking the cable car to the top of Table Mountain
- Hiking along the spectacular Wild Coast
- Stargazing in Sutherland
- Snorkelling in Sodwana
- Hiking in the Drakensberg

Don't bother with ...

- Sandboarding down a Johannesburg mine dump

Best water-based adventures

- Do the Duzi
- Dive the Aliwal Shoal along the KwaZulu-Natal South Coast
- Take part in the Trans Aghulas Challenge (the world's toughest inflatable boat race)
- Swim the Midmar Mile
- Go on an Air Jaws photographic safari to Seal Island
- Kiteboard at Langebaan
- The Robben Island swim
- Go boating during the sardine run
- Dive the chokka beds at Cape St Francis
- Dive the *HMS Birkenhead* at Danger Point in Struisbaai

Don't bother with . . .

- The Wave House in Durban, unless you've just hit puberty with a vengeance.

Best airborne adventures

- Abseil Signal Hill
- Paraglide over Du Toitskloof Mountains
- See the whales over Walker Bay from a biplane
- Fly in a Tiger Moth over Egoli (or a DC3 Dakota or DC4 Skymaster)
- Fly over the Cradle of Humankind in a hot-air balloon
- Fly in a fighter jet from Thunder City Cape Town
- Learn to fly at Port Alfred 43 Air School

Best cycle routes

- The Cape Argus Pick n Pay cycle route
- Helshoogte Pass from Stellenbosch to Franschhoek
- Suikerbosrand
- Cycle the largest meteorite crater in the world at the Vredefort Dome
- Long Tom Pass
- Midlands Meander

Don't bother with . . .

- The annual naked bike race organised by South Africa's naturist community – all too painful for words (and definitely not easy on the eye)

Best hiking trails

- The Otter Trail
- Eden to Addo Mega Hike
- Wild Coast beach hikes
- The Dolphin Trail
- Olifants River Backpack Trail in the Kruger National Park
- Slaying the Dragon in the Drakensberg
- Oystercatcher Trail, Mosselbay
- Two River Trail, Eastern Cape
- Suikerbosrand (especially for city slickers)

Don't bother with . . .

- Hoerikwaggo Tented Classic if you're into all pain and no gain, this slick trail has Sherpas carrying all your worldly goods

Best fishing spots

- Dullstroom, Mpumalanga
- The Rhodes District
- Du Toitskloof, Western Cape
- Jonkershoek Valley, Stellenbosch
- Elephant Coast
- Chrissiesmeer
- Cape Point
- Wild Coast

Best surfing spots

- Tubes at Jeffreys Bay
- Dungeons, Hout Bay
- Cave Rock, The Bluff
- Kalk Bay Reef
- Nahoon Reef, East London
- Victoria Bay
- Walker Bay, Hermanus
- The Kom, Noordhoek

Beware of . . .

- Kalk Bay during enormous swells brought on by the southeaster, unless you have balls of steel.

Urban
DISTRACTIONS

Cape Town is considered one of the greatest cities in the world. Travel magazines from *National Geographic Traveler* to *Condé Nast* have consistently voted it amongst the top three in the world and the best in Africa. Johannesburg, or Jozi to those who live there, is regarded by those in the know as the most vibrant city on the continent, though some will say it has yet to lose its mining-camp aspect. Pretoria is where most of the embassies are found and it has a cosmopolitan, sophisticated feel. People in Durban and Port Elizabeth are friendly and so laid back they sometimes appear to have smoked too much of the magic herb for which the areas in which they are located are famous.

Best places to chill

- Long Street in Cape Town – a great alternative to those not turned on by the V&A Waterfront
- Vilakazi Street in Soweto – the best of township style
- 4th Avenue in Parkhurst – a real village street close to the heart of Johannesburg
- Florida Road in Durban – perfectly captures this laid-back city. Great restaurants and clubs too
- Hatfield in Pretoria – cosmopolitan and fun in this often staid city
- Beach Road in Port Elizabeth – everything on offer without the glitz
- Newtown in Johannesburg – for the creative energy
- The Esplanade in Durban, especially the Bat Centre – the views over one of the most beautiful harbours on earth are spectacular

- The Promenade section of Beach Road in Sea Point, Cape Town – intimate eateries, after which you can stroll one of the most romantic places in the city
- Clifton in Cape Town – for the jet set

Don't bother with . . .

- East London – unless you are looking for a hooker in a grimy port city
- 7th Street in Melville, Johannesburg – unless you are looking for drugs
- Pietermaritzburg – unless you are wanting a good rest in what is deservedly known as 'sleepy hollow'
- Durban beachfront – unless you like crowds and hobos asking for cash
- Bloemfontein – unless you like being bored out of your skull, other than for the fabulous Mystic Boer
- Kimberley – unless you are into great architecture, history and ghosts (who are free to roam when the city completely shuts up shop at sundown)

Avoid

- Rustenburg and Polokwane – get the hell out as fast as you can unless you like 70s architecture and hillbillies

SMALL TOWNS

South Africa, like everywhere else, has both beautiful small towns and horrible dumps. The three oldest towns in the country are

of interesting ghost towns dating back to the Great Trek and the
Eastern Escarpment gold rush.

Great Trek Ghost Towns

The tall, autocratic Voortrekker leader Andries Hendrik Potgieter,
known as 'Ou Blauberg' (Old Blue Mountain), led his people
from the Cape in 1835 and established Potchefstroom, the first
town in the then Transvaal. But its distance from the east coast
ports and creeping British influence forced him to once again
pack up and in June 1845 he settled in a well-watered valley on
the Eastern Escarpment about four kilometres north of present-
day Ohrigstad. There he built a fort, around which a village of
mud brick and thatch buildings mushroomed. This he named
Andries-Ohrigstad, after himself and Amsterdam merchant
Georgius Gerardus Ohrig, who was well disposed to the trekkers
and had sent supplies for them to Delagoa Bay.

At about the same time the British annexed Natal, causing the
Boers there to again trek into the interior, with one group under
JJ Burger arriving at Andries-Ohrigstad. Within a short time
Potgieter and the new arrivals clashed to the point of civil war over
leadership and governance. This was exacerbated by a devastating
outbreak of malaria, which forced the abandonment of the town.
Today only a part of the walling of the old fort is preserved.

The Boers allied to the Burger faction moved south to found
Lydenburg, while Potgieter took a small commando to the Orange
Free State to support the Boers there. The rest of his party under

Jan Valentyn Botha moved north to the foot of the Soutpansberg range, where they established the autonomous republic of Zoutpansberg Maatschappij with the kapsteil (A-frame) and reed-hutted town of Zoutpansbergdorp as its capital. This soon developed into a chaotic, brawling haunt for hunters and all sorts of renegades seeking the anonymity of a frontier. It became worse after the truculent Stephanus Schoeman became leader in 1855 after Potgieter and his son died in quick succession. Changing the name of the capital to Schoemansdal, he let it descend into anarchy. Cattle rustling, various outrages and overhunting led to direct conflict with the Venda nation that escalated into war in 1867. The Transvaal sent a commando of 400 men to support Schoeman, but it was unsuccessful and the Venda attacked and destroyed Schoemansdal on 15 July. About 20 kilometres from Makhado (Louis Trichardt) on the road to Vivo, all that remains of the town are a number of rebuilt frontier houses that form part of a national monument.

Eastern Escarpment Ghost Towns

(From *Ghost Towns of South Africa*, Pat Hopkins)

As the alluvial diamonds in the Kimberley area became harder and harder to find in the 1870s, so many diggers began packing their meagre belongings to join the new rush to the Eastern Escarpment of the Transvaal Republic where news was filtering through of the discovery of gold. It was time to head off for a new Eldorado.

The existence of gold in the interior of southern Africa had long been suspected, driven by fanciful legends of King Solomon's

Mines and the land of Monomotapa that was fabulously endowed with the precious metal. Prospectors had begun scouring the Transvaal in the early 1860s, but it was not until February 1873 when Tom McLachlan made promising finds in a gully on the slopes of Spitskop near Hendriksdal that real interest began to develop.

Other finds soon followed and the community of prospectors began to expand. Then, in September, 'Wheelbarrow' Alex Patterson packed his belongings on his handcart and broke away from the main concentration of miners to follow the course of a river. His instincts proved correct and he came upon the first payable yield in the region. When another prospector, William Trafford, saw what Patterson had discovered, he whooped 'The Pilgrim is at rest!'

It was the greatest rush since the Klondike and ragtag hordes descended in their thousands on Pilgrim's Rest. There was, however, no tranquillity among these hopefuls chasing their dreams first here and then south to Barberton when Auguste Robert, nicknamed French Bob, found the Pioneer Reef on the south-east side of the De Kaap Valley in June 1883 and Edwin Bray revealed rich deposits of gold in the Valley of Death in 1885 when hacking at a vine with a machete.

'A carrion crowlike gathering,' moaned French Bob of the ensuing rush. 'They came to snatch the spoil from the hands of the toil-worn ragged men who had hunted and brought down the prey.'

The gold that Edwin Bray's panga revealed turned out to be

Sheba Reef – the richest single find of the yellow metal in history. This strike sparked the shortest, wildest gold boom ever and new mines – including New Chum, Twice Rejected, Nil Desperadum, Gould's Salvation, Joe's Luck, Honeybird Creek and Lost Ten Tribes – quickly opened near Bray's Golden Quarry. Over 100 companies, offering nearly five shares for every ounce of gold, were soon floated on the two stock exchanges in nearby Barberton.

Things were even wilder at Eureka City atop a hill near Barberton. Prospectors arrived by the score, among them the colourful Bob Buck, Spanish Joe, Black Sam, Wally the Soldier, Dirty Dick and Great Bonanza. The town began when Durban businessman J Sherwood opened a butchery and the Queen of Sheba Hotel, named in honour of his famously ugly wife, who was jokingly compared to the impossibly beautiful monarch of legend. Soon there was a racetrack and innumerable saloons that radiated light, music, laughter and gunshots by night. Most popular was the Red Light Canteen, where Cockney Liz was auctioned every Saturday night – once receiving 100 Kimberley Imperial shares worth £2 000 for her services.

'Gold fever' was even more evident at Jamestown near Barberton and Steynsdorp in the Umhlondosi Valley on the Swaziland border – the latter becoming synonymous with speculation and the fraudulent salting of claims. Pockets of gold were found in the valley by Jim Painter and Frank Austen in July 1885 and in no time there were 800 diggers working what was known as the New Paarl Goldfields, centred around Painter's Camp, which became Steynsburg then Steysdorp after government representative Commandant JP Steyn. At its peak this turbulent town had two newspapers, *The Phoenix* and the *Steynsdorp Observer*; a bank; a prison; shops selling mining supplies, dynamite and guns; six hotels; and 30 pubs featuring the flashiest barmaids serving Hollands Squareface Gin and cheap Cape brandy from oak barrels to the assorted boozers, gamblers, confidence tricksters and petty crooks who gravitated here.

But the end came quickly, and by 1887 the prospectors had left for the new finds on the Witwatersrand to the west and the Murchison Range to the north; the Barberton stock exchanges had collapsed; and Eureka City, Jamestown and Steynsdorp had become ghost towns.

In 1870 prospectors Edward Button and James Sutherland had found non-payable deposits of gold in the mountains round present-day Gravelotte. They named these the Murchison Range after English geologist Sir Roderick Murchison. In 1886 Auguste Robert found a richer seam in the area, which became known as the Selati Gold Fields and a new rush started for French Bob's Camp that was changed to Leydsdorp in 1890 after Transvaal state secretary WJ Leyds. Here the excesses of the other mining towns were magnified as canteens, bars and hotels sprang up overnight. It too had its own newspaper, the *Leydsdorp Leader*. And the swindling was so bad that a new saying emerged: 'You get a liar, a damn liar, and a prospector of the Murchison Range.' The greatest scam was perpetrated by Belgians Baron Eugene Oppenheim and his brother Robert, who floated the Selati Railway Company in Brussels in 1892. The railway was supposed to link Leydsdorp with the Pretoria-Lourenço Marques line at Komatipoort, but the brothers were more concerned with fleecing

European investors with an ever-lengthening line that eventually twisted to nowhere through the present Kruger National Park and surrounding reserves.

As the gold petered out so Leydsdorp died and by 1924 it was a ghost town. Efforts are being made to restore the village to its former glory, but it remains true that the busiest part of the town is the well-populated graveyard.

Best of small-town South Africa

- Franschhoek in the Western Cape for its stunning beauty and fine restaurants
- Nieu Bethesda in the Eastern Cape for the Owl House
- McGregor in the Western Cape for its artists
- Parys in the Free State for being fabulously pink in a drab region
- Knysna in the Western Cape, but please do more to uplift the poor, who appear invisible here
- Tulbagh in the Western Cape for being so pretty
- Matjiesfontein in the Western Cape for being so eccentric; ditto Agatha near Tzaneen
- Groot Marico in North West for mampoer and being Groot Marico
- Swellendam in the Western Cape for great architecture
- Prince Albert in the Western Cape for its setting and Karoo houses
- Arniston and Elim in the Western Cape for fishermen's cottages
- Barberton in Mpumalanga for its colourful houses and

characters

- Kaapschehoop in Mpumalanga for its wild horses and mist
- Graskop in Mpumalanga for the incredible Graskop Hotel, South Africa's first art hotel
- Clarens in the Free State, albeit a tad twee

Avoid

- Port Nolloth in the Northern Cape – ugly weather, ugly place, ugly people
- Mussina in Limpopo – brutish border town that would make anything between the United States and Mexico appear tame
- Port St Johns in the Eastern Cape – a Zombieville time warp of ageing, toothless hippies with faded tattoos and even more faded memories
- Hopetown in the Northern Cape – place without hope (with acknowledgment to Chris Marais)
- Beauty in Limpopo – the most misnamed place on the planet
- Mafikeng in North West – OhmiGod dirty and depressing
- Vryburg in North West – absolutely horrid
- Newcastle – a coal-mining, industrial scar on the landscape
- Pofadder in the Northern Cape – venomously appalling
- Ventersdorp in North West – unrepentantly racist, it has been earmarked as the administration hole should the world ever be given an enema
- Mtubatuba in KwaZulu-Natal – the name evokes an African drum, but this place is more like one of those

tin drums given to the children of your worst enemy at Christmas
- Aliwal North in the Eastern Cape – a Flat Earth kind of place where the Dutch Reformed Church has decreed that Earth is the centre of the universe and that the sun revolves around it
- The arc of coal-mining towns from Sasolburg to Witbank – the air quality is amongst the worst in the world and the region makes Wales look pretty

ZOOS

While we do not want to enter the debate on the ethicacy of zoos, the National Zoological Gardens in the heart of Pretoria is considered one of the top three in the world. It does fantastic work with highly endangered species and has impressive holding areas. The Johannesburg Zoo is also worth a visit. For the rest, they range from poor to appalling and should not be supported.

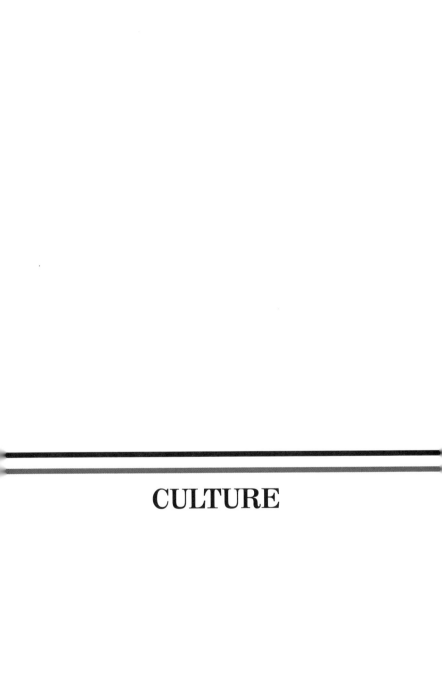

CULTURE

To understand the wealth of creativity of this country one just needs to look at our exquisite arts and crafts. At any roadside stall or craft centre you will find basketware, beadwork, wire goods, embroidery and wooden carvings. Sure, there is a lot of copycat 'junk' out there, but the real arts and crafts inspired by African traditions are beautiful pieces of work that deserve to be treasured.

Best arts and crafts

- Ardmore Ceramic Art in KwaZulu-Natal – for the best, most vibrant ceramics in Africa. More fine art than arts and crafts
- Monkeybiz ceramics in the Western Cape – fun stuff made by locally trained artists. No two pieces the same
- Zulu beadwork, beaded dolls, jewellery and ilala palm baskets – great for decor
- Traditional Xhosa outfits and *shwe shwe* fabrics – recently discovered by couturiers
- Wire cars – great gifts for boys of all ages
- Ndebele fabrics, beaded bracelets, pottery and necklaces – works of art
- Venda pottery, wood sculptures and drums – inspired by the spirit world
- Junkyard art, especially that from the Mofolo Art Centre in Soweto – a creative statement about the value of things we discard
- Sotho blankets and conical straw hats – useful and colourful

- Nguni hides – colourful cattle skins used for ethnic decor if you are into using dead animal parts. Preferable to wild animal skins

Don't bother with . . .

- Big Five arts and crafts along the road to Kruger – very kitsch
- Anything made from an ostrich or ostrich egg – even more kitsch
- Anything made from a wild animal – shame on you

Best places to buy arts and crafts

- Along the Ribolla Open Africa Route in Venda, Limpopo
- Greenmarket Square in Cape Town
- Rosebank African Market in Johannesburg
- Rosebank Rooftop Market in Johannesburg
- Art Africa in Parkview, Umhlanga Rocks and Knysna
- Delagoa Trading in Graskop, Pretoria, Dullstroom and the V&A Waterfront
- St George's Park in Port Elizabeth
- Mai Mai Market/Bazaar in Johannesburg
- Pan African Market in Long Street in Cape Town
- Shangana Cultural Village near Hazyview in Mpumalanga

Don't bother with . . .

- The Hillfox Market in Johannesburg – unless you like awful pop stars like Kurt Darren and Patricia Lewis
- Bruma Flea Market – unless you like cheap Eastern junk

South Africa's musical heritage includes an eclectic span of influences from traditional African to European and American. It all started with the Khoisan and their basic harps, *ramkie* (a makeshift guitar) and the *mamokhorong* (a single string violin).

After the Europeans arrived, Western music filtered into the Cape and was played by slave orchestras and travelling musicians. The early missionaries played a major role in the development of music in South Africa and today gospel and choral mass voice are extremely popular. In the early nineteenth century, music in the Cape received a new dimension with travelling minstrel shows of white performers with painted black faces singing spiritual tunes from the American South. By the 1830s real African American minstrel troupes arrived and their legacy lives on in the Cape Minstrels (and the Kaapse Klopse carnival that begins every year in Cape Town on 2 January).

The minstrel influence helped to develop what we know as *isicathamiya*, a music form that has received international recognition. The sounds of *marabi* developed in the early twentieth century with the urbanisation of the migrant black workforce who lived in townships, hostels and ghettos. This music, a keyboard style with deep African traditions, was played in shebeens and was hugely popular in the 1930s and 40s. Over the decades *marabi* influenced *mbaqanga* and *kwela*, a form of jazz that with its pennywhistle brought international acclaim to artists such as Spokes Mashiyane. In places like Sophiatown *mbaqanga* jazz brought fame to the likes of the Three Jazzamolos and solo artists such as Dolly Rathebe, Letta Mbulu and Miriam Makeba.

Cross-cultural influences and the political landscape after 1948 continued to influence South African musicians and new forms began to develop under the likes of Gideon Nxumalo and Todd Matshikiza, whose musical *King Kong* travelled abroad to critical acclaim. During this time, many of South Africa's best musicians went into exile, where they further honed their skills. Among these were Abdullah Ibrahim, Jonas Gwangwa, Letta Mbulu, Hugh Masakela and Caiphas Semenya.

In more recent years South African musicians have taken African jazz in new directions. The 80s saw the rise of Afro-jazz bands, which married American influences to home-grown sounds. The sounds of imported rap and hip-hop are also evident in the township form of house music, *kwaito*, which emerged in the 1990s.

Music trivia

- Eric Gallo, an agent for Brunswick Records, established the first recording studio in South Africa in 1932 when he converted a basement below a Johannesburg cinema.

Did you know?

Impoverished Zulu migrant
worker Solomon Linda produced

'Mbube' in 1939, which would become one of the most plagiarised songs in history with over 160 uncredited cover versions. Best known as 'The Lion Sleeps Tonight' and Pete Seeger's 'Wimowhey', it has earned $15 million in royalties, but not for the composer, who died virtually penniless in 1962. His daughters settled for an undisclosed sum with the American copyright holders in 2006.

- Miriam Makeba, known as Mama Afrika, in 1966 won the Grammy together with Harry Belafonte for Best Folk Recording for *An Evening With Belafonte/Makeba*.
- In the mid-1980s the Alternative Afrikaans Music Movement emerged, which culminated in the Voëlvry tour of 1989 that liberated Afrikaner youth from the paternalism of the past and helped pave their embrace of the coming new South Africa.
- *Isicathamiya* group Ladysmith Black Mambazo won their first Grammy for Best Traditional Folk Recording for *Shaka Zulu* produced by Paul Simon in 1987. They would win again in 2005 and 2009.
- The Dave Matthews Band formed by South African-born Dave Matthews won the Grammy for Best Rock Performance by a Duo or Group with Vocal for 'So Much to Say' in 1995. They would win again in 2004.
- The Soweto Gospel Choir won the Grammy for Best Traditional World Music Album in 2007. They would

triumph again in 2008. The 26-member group was formed to celebrate the inspirational power of African gospel music.

DANCE

South Africa has its own form of dance expression in pantsula, which emerged in the 1950s. This was much more than just a dance – it was a lifestyle, a fashion statement, a way of being that fermented on township streets of places like Alexandra and Sophiatown. It has evolved into diverse modern-day forms and expression.

The low point of South African dance came in 1973 in the ultra-conservative town of Volksrust at the height of suffocating repressive social mores when stripper Glenda Kemp, aided by her python Thinpy, did a reverse strip by arriving starkers on stage before proceeding to dress. This would have been bad enough at the time had she not also chosen to do this performance as a nubile Zulu maiden – for which she wore black body paint and an Afro wig.

The high point came in March 2009 when dancer/choreographer Robyn Orlin received the Ordre National du Mérite, the French National Order of Merit for her contribution to the arts.

RADIO, FILM AND TELEVISION

South Africa has a vibrant radio, film and television industry, despite lack of funds and support.

- The Cinematograph of Londoner Robert Paul was the first cinema show in South Africa on 11 May 1896.
- The first feature-length film, *The Great Kimberley Diamond Robbery*, was made in 1910 by the Springbok Production Company.
- Dr Hendrik van der Bijl invented the thermionic valve in 1914, on which all broadcasting and television depended until the advent of digital technology. He also developed the scrambling device for radio speech.
- The South African Railways and Harbours made the first commercial radio broadcast in the country, on 18 December 1923. The following year independent services began broadcasting from Cape Town and Durban. Unable to financially sustain themselves, they were taken over by the Schlesinger organisation and incorporated into the African Broadcasting Company on 1 April 1927. When they were still not viable, the government took over the service and renamed it the South African Broadcasting Commission (SABC) in 1936.
- African Film Productions in 1930 produced the first South African 'talkies'.
- FM radio transmissions began from Johannesburg in 1961.
- On 5 January 1976 South Africa belatedly entered the television age after six months of test transmissions.
- South Africa's most successful film, *The Gods Must Be Crazy* directed by Jamie Uys, was released in 1980.
- Charlize Theron became the first South African to win an Oscar for Best Actress in February 2004. Born in Benoni, her portrayal of prostitute and serial killer Aileen Wuornos in the

film *Monster*, for which she had to put on 13 kilograms, had already garnered her 14 awards.
- *Son of Man* was the first South African film to be entered in the prestigious Sundance Film Festival.
- *Tsotsi* became the first movie from South Africa to win the Oscar for Best Foreign Language Film, on 5 March 2006. Directed by Gavin Hood, it starred Presley Chweneyagae as a township thug.

Major films shot on location in South Africa

- *Blood Diamond*
- *Catch a Fire*
- *Lord of War*
- *Hotel Rwanda*
- *Drum*
- *Racing Stripes*
- *Stander*
- *The Scorpion King 2*
- *Invictus*
- *District 9*

Infamous moments on South African television

- The 10 seconds of pornography inserted by a technician into a news bulletin in 1986. This was followed by an announcement: 'We have a problem. Please do not adjust your set'
- State President PW Botha's hijacking of the news to

- News reader Colin Fluxman breaking down on *Good Morning South Africa* in July 1990 when it dawned on him that the woman caught in a compromising position at the Peninsula Hotel with political activist and priest Dr Allan Boesak was his wife

THEATRE

South African theatre has grown out of European, American and African storytelling traditions. Until the musical *King Kong*, in 1959, local theatre mainly consisted of imported productions. The real explosion came in 1974 when Barney Simon and Manny Manim launched Johannesburg's Market Theatre, which brought together formal theatre and black talent as a force for change. Today there are over a hundred theatres in the country.

The first formal theatre production in South Africa was in 1838 in Grahamstown with the performance of Andrew Geddes Bain's *Kekkelbek or Life Among the Hottentots*. At the same time the traditions of the theatre were being introduced to indigenous populations by missionaries as a form of education. This was taken from rural areas to the townships that developed after the discovery of diamonds and gold, and theatre began to flourish there in the 1920s.

The Methethwe Lucky Stars troupe was formed in 1929 and the Bantu Dramatic Society in 1932. In 1937 *The Girl Who Killed to Save* by Herbert Dhlomo was the first published play by a black writer. In the mid-60s Gibson Kente took a theatre troupe on the road touring townships. Among the actors were Percy

Mtwa and Mbongeni Ngema, who came up with the country's greatest theatre success, *Woza Albert!* This would go on to win the Fringe First Award at the Edinburgh Festival, the San Francisco Bay Area Theatre Critics Circle Award, the Los Angeles Drama Critics Award, the British Theatre Association Award and the Obie Award.

During the Struggle for Freedom, theatre became one of the most important mediums of expression. The forerunner to The Market Theatre in giving voice to the oppressed was the fringe The Space Theatre in Cape Town, which opened in 1972 and performed to multiracial audiences. The Market Theatre and the Baxter Theatre in Cape Town, which opened in 1977, followed this tradition after The Space closed. They, in turn, would nurture some of South Africa's finest playwriting talent, including Welcome Msomi, Zakes Mda, Maishe Maponya and Matsemela Manaka. John Kani, one of the most formidable acting talents to have come out of South Africa and known as the grandfather of South African Theatre, is perhaps most famous for his protest plays performed during the apartheid years, where along with Athol Fugard and Winston Ntshona, his name is celebrated for *Sizwe Banzi is Dead* and *The Island*.

Did you know?

John Kani's role in *Miss Julie* in Cape Town in 1982 caused a massive controversy when he kissed a white woman on stage. He subsequently received death threats and landed up in hospital after an attacker stabbed him 11 times.

Best theatres

- The Market Theatre in Johannesburg
- The Baxter Theatre in Cape Town
- The Artscape Theatre Centre in Cape Town
- The State Theatre in Pretoria
- Theatre on the Bay in Camps Bay, Cape Town
- The Playhouse in Durban
- Joburg Theatre Complex

Best festivals

- National Arts Festival in Grahamstown
- Klein Karoo Nasionale Kunstefees in Oudtshoorn
- Aardklop in Potchefstroom
- Arts Alive in Johannesburg
- Innibos in Nelspruit

Don't bother with . . .

- Any of the Barnyard Theatres or casino-type theatres who serve up commercial drivel and call it theatre

Beauty queen trivia

- Penny Coelen became the first South African to wear the Miss World crown in 1958. Anneline Kriel won by default in 1974 when British winner Helen Morgan was stripped of the title. In 1993 and 1994, South Africa's first black contestants, Jacqui Mofokeng and Basetsane Makgalemele were respectively first runners-up. The only South African to win the Miss Universe title was Margaret Gardiner in 1978

LITERATURE

South African literary milestones:

- *The Story of an African Farm* written by Olive Schreiner was published in 1883 to international acclaim. In 1908 she formed the Women's Enfranchisement League in Cape Town.

Did you know?

Olive Schreiner's *The Story of an African Farm* first appeared under the pen name of Ralph Iron, as female authors were still battling for acceptance.

- *Mhudi* by Sol Plaatje in 1930 was the first published novel by a black South African. He was instrumental in founding the forerunner to the ANC, the South African Native National Congress.
- *Cry, the Beloved Country* by Alan Paton was published in 1948.
- *The Lord of the Rings* by Bloemfontein-born JRR Tolkien was published in London, where he lived, in 1954.
- *Supernature* by Johannesburg-born zoologist and botanist Lyall Watson was published in 1973. In the 1960s he was director of the Johannesburg Zoo. He died in 2008 in Australia.

- Nadine Gordimer won the Nobel Prize for Literature in 1991.
- JM Coetzee won the Nobel Prize for Literature in 2003. He now lives in Australia.

FOOD AND DRINK

Food

South African cuisine is generally a fusion of all the diverse influences of those who have chosen to make the country their home. But there are some dishes that are unique to our shores, including:

- *Amanqina* – boiled and spiced hoof of cow, pig or sheep.
- *Biltong* – a much better version of jerky or dried meat. All three authors are vegetarian, but this is the one thing we all miss.
- *Bobotie* – a slightly sweeter, spicier version of shepherd's pie. And a damn sight better.
- *Boerewors* – is a long, fat sausage containing beef, pork and spices. It is an essential of the braaivleis, the local variant of the barbeque.
- *Bredie* – a stew of meat (usually mutton), vegetable and spices cooked slowly for a long time.
- *Bunny chow* – a South African dish developed by Indians in Durban. It is a half or full loaf of hollowed bread stuffed with curry. An everyman dish that is delicious and messy.
- *Frikkadel* – local meatball.

- *Green mielies* – white maize roasted in its leaves over an open fire. Mainly purchased from street vendors.
- *Koeksisters* – syrupy, very sweet plaited dough.
- *Konfyt* – chunks of fruit soaked in lime water then cooked in syrup and spices before bottling. Hard fruits are used in this very sweet preserve, especially melon, quince and green fig.
- *Mala* – boiled then fried chicken intestines.
- *Maotwana* – cleaned, salted chicken feet boiled then fried. Also known as walkie-talkies.
- *Mielie meal* – a robust version of couscous used in everything from dumplings to a stiff porridge known as pap.
- *Melktert* – a Dutch-influenced milk tart.
- *Mogodu* – boiled tripe usually served with pap or samp and beans.
- *Mopane worms* – first dried, then fried, these are only for the most adventurous of palates.
- *Morogo* – wild spinach; absolutely delicious.
- *Potjiekos* – meat, vegetables and spices layered in a three-legged cast-iron pot and cooked over an open fire.
- *Rooibos tea* – a herbal tea from *Cyclopia genistoides* bush.
- *Rusks* – a hard biscuit made from dried bread portions. Especially delicious are those flavoured with buttermilk.
- *Samoosas* – a deep-fried triangular pastry filled with spiced meat or vegetables, made by the Indian community.
- *Skop* – a township staple of braised cow, sheep or goat head, eaten on the bone.
- *Snoek* – a fish found along the Cape coast. Normally braaied or smoked. Very bony, very salty, very nice.
- *Sosaties* – skewered marinated meat usually grilled or cooked on the braai.
- *Sweet vegetables* – an Afrikaner staple is to cook vegetables

with syrup, honey or dried fruit.

- *Umngqusho* – samp and beans.
- *Waterblommetjie bredie* – waterblommetjies are a creamy white flower found in the waterways of the Western Cape. They are used in stews with meat, especially mutton, and sorrel.

Don't bother with . . .

- *Melkkos* – an old Boer concoction of bread and milk that should have died with the Voortrekkers
- *Bokkoms* – dried, very salty small silver fish. Found on the West Coast, they are truly horrible, though a very good purgative

Wine

In 1652 the Dutch East India Company dispatched Jan van Riebeeck to erect a fort and lay out a garden in Table Bay. Five years later the first Free Burgher farmers were released to work their own land and in 1659 Van Riebeeck recorded the making of the first wine at the Cape. From then on Cape Town would be known to successive explorers and sailors as the Tavern of the Seas.

The South African wine industry is still heavily focused in this region, now the Western Cape. With its Mediterranean climate, soils and the influence of the Atlantic and Indian Oceans' air, it is ideal for grape growing. The first wines were made from indigenous wild grapes, but later French vines were planted – probably chenin blanc and muscat.

The industry received a huge boost in 1686, when a large number of Huguenot religious refugees arrived from France after the revocation of the Edict of Nantes. Most of them originated from wine-growing regions, bringing with them their knowledge and skills. Many chose to live in what is now Franschhoek near Stellenbosch, their farms still linked to France through names such as La Motte, Cabrière, Provence and Dieu Donné.

In 1866 the winelands were devastated by phylloxera, the vine root-killing bug. This led to a massive replanting of the winelands, which laid the foundation for the current industry structure of cooperatives and private producers. These cater for the entire spectrum from everyday consumption to high-end quality wines, many of which have won international acclaim.

While most of the grapes from the winelands will be familiar to visitors, there is one uniquely South African viticultural cross: pinotage. Bred by Professor Abraham Perold at Stellenbosch University in 1925 from pinot noir and cinsaut, it produces a deep red wine with smoky, earthy flavours. It is also often blended or made into fortified and sparkling wines.

Historic Wine Estates

Groot Constantia

Groot Constantia is renowned for its quality wines, which visitors can taste at the estate. But it is so much more than that.

Simon van der Stel arrived at the Cape as commander in 1679 and soon after was appointed the first governor of the settlement.

Six years later he was given the right to select for himself a tract of land to use for his own purposes. After an extensive investigation he chose 'the heatherlands, morasses, wheat and woodlands' of a valley he named Constantia.

Here he began planting thousands of vines, orchards and oak trees, and building the first of the great Cape homesteads, the Groot Constantia manor house that is now one of the leading tourist attractions of the region. Accessed along an avenue of oaks, the thatched Dutch and German-inspired house features gables, dungeons and a stone bath in which slaves washed their feet during grape pressing. The wine cellar with the pediment depicting Ganymede and Bacchus was added later. After his death in 1712, the estate was divided into three: Groot Constantia winelands, Klein Constantia and Buitenverwachting.

Did you know?

Groot Constantia is the oldest wine estate in South Africa.

Vergelegen

Wine magazine has consistently voted Vergelegen Wine Estate in Somerset West the best winery in South Africa. It was acquired and developed by the son of Simon van der Stel, Willem Adriaan, who succeeded his father as governor of the Cape.

Five of the Chinese camphors at the entrance to the manor house have been documented as the oldest living trees on the subcontinent and were declared a national monument in 1942. The Cape Dutch house was so big and opulent that it incurred the wrath of the Free Burghers of the colony, leading to the recall of the governor to Holland in 1708. When it was purchased by Anglo American Farms in 1987, the mansion was extensively refurbished and decorated with early Cape furniture and objects that told of its 300 year existence.

Boschendal

Boschendal wine farm is planted with Sauvignon blanc and Chardonnay, but it is for its award-winning noble red varietals that it is renowned. The modern winery incorporates the original cellar for Le Rhone Manor House built in 1795. Here the past blends with the future as winemakers use cutting-edge technology to make award-winning wines.

The majestic Boschendal (Wood and Dale) wine farm in the Drakenstein Valley was planted with vines in the late 1680s by Jean le Long, a Huguenot refugee. But the place was occupied long before as attested by artefacts found on the mountain slopes dating back to the Early, Middle and Late Stone Ages. This Franschhoek wine farm was bought by the Huguenot Abraham de Villiers in 1717. He was from Champagne then La Rochelle in France before fleeing to Holland, where he was recruited for his wine-growing expertise.

In 1746 Jean de Villiers built a house on this Franschhoek wine estate that over the centuries developed into a typical but magnificent H-frame Cape Dutch mansion with external wooden shutters. Soon after acquiring it in 1969, Anglo American restored the house. With baroque and neo-classical touches it is furnished in the early Cape tradition, making it one of the few such authentic

buildings open to the public in the region. Of particular interest
are the old-fashioned rose garden and the friezes exposed during
the refurbishment.

Wine Routes

Stellenbosch Wine Route

Stellenbosch is considered to be the capital of the South African
wine industry. With over 60 estates, it is the leading centre for
viticulture and viticulture research. It has the oldest wine route
in the country, where visitors can taste the produce of more than
40 estates. Based on the French Route de Vin and German wine
routes, it was launched in 1971.

Did you know?

The Constantia wine route, which
takes in amongst others the three
Cape Town estates of Groot
Constantia, Klein Constantia and
Buitenverwachting, is the shortest
in South Africa and probably the
world.

Paarl Wine Route

The Paarl winelands are just to the north of Stellenbosch and
are framed by the majestic Groot and Klein Drakenstein and
Franschhoek mountains. Running through the Paarl wine estates
is the Berg River, which sustains the winelands as the area is
dependent on irrigation. While it produces fine Chardonnays,
Sauvignon blancs and Rieslings, it is legendary for its international

award-winning noble reds. That is why the Paarl wine route is affectionately known as the 'Red Route'.

Franschhoek Wine Route

The Franschhoek winelands, set in a tranquil valley, are where some of South Africa's best wines are produced. At its heart is Franschhoek (French Corner), which many consider to be the most beautiful small town in the country. Around the town are more than 40 wine farms, many of which belong to the Vignerons de Franschhoek wine route. These offer a superb variety from white wines such as Chardonnay to noble reds like Shiraz and Merlot. Then there are the valley's signature Methode Cap Classique sparkling wines. And the harvest of the Franschhoek winelands is celebrated with the Franschhoek Oesfees – a festival of food and music at Solms-Delta Wine Estate in April.

Worcester Wine Route

Worcester is the largest wine-growing district in South Africa, producing nearly a quarter of the country's wine and brandy. Named after the Marquis of Worcester, the brother of governor Lord Charles Somerset, Worcester is a baby in comparison to other towns in the province. It was laid out on two farms in 1819 as a sub-drostdy of nearby Tulbagh, only receiving municipal status in 1922. But since then it has grown rapidly to become the business centre of the Breede River Valley. This is due in large part to its being home to the world's largest brandy distillery at KWV. In the area are 24 cooperatives, three private wineries and two brandy cellars, most of which are open to the public for tastings, along the Worcester wine route that meanders through the verdant valley enclosed by mountain ranges.

Route 62 is the longest wine
route in the world.

Best wine estates

- Groot Constantia – it is so beautiful one almost forgets its great wines
- Rustenberg – for great reds
- Boschendal – renowned for its manor house, restaurant and red wines
- Backsberg – for consistently good wines at realistic prices
- Thelema – has set the bar for what the country can produce
- Villiera – cannot be beaten for value and quality, especially their bubblies, which regularly outscore French Champagnes in blind tastings
- Tokara – at the crest of the Helshoogte Pass, it has great wines and a fine restaurant featuring its own olive oils
- Haute Cabrière – in the breathtaking Franschhoek Valley, it offers everything from great views to fine bubblies and the eccentricities of its owner
- Vergelegen – consistently voted by *Wine* magazine as the best estate in the country, it has much more to offer with fine restaurants and a well-restored manor house
- Morgenster – known for its Bordeaux-style wines, it also makes some of the country's best olive oil
- Fairview Estate – for its white wines, goat's milk cheeses and restaurant
- Waterford – enjoy award-winning wines in a tranquil setting

Don't bother with . . .

- Spier if you are anti-commercialism; the place is known as the Disneyland of local wine

Beer

African Beer

There are a number of variants of African beer, which was brewed long before the arrival of Europeans. The most popular is *umqombothi* made from maize, sorghum and yeast. Millet can also be used.

Clear Beer

European-style beers have been brewed in South Africa since the arrival of the Dutch in 1652. South African Breweries was founded in 1895 by Jacob Letterstedt and today completely dominates the local market. In 2002 it became the second largest brewery in the world when it merged with the Miller Brewing Company to form SABMiller. That is enough about SAB, as there are far better local beers to be enjoyed.

Best South African brewers

- Gilroy's Brewery in Johannesburg – its Gilroy Serious dark ale was judged best beer in the southern hemisphere and second best in the world at a blind tasting
- Birkenhead Brewery near Stanford in the Western Cape – there are some that swear their beers are

better than Gilroy's, but not many
- Nottingham Road Brewing Company at Rawdon's Hotel in Nottingham Road, KwaZulu-Natal – their beers named Tiddly Toad, Pye-eyed Possum, Whistling Weasel and Pickled Pig are a treat
- Firkin Hophouse Micro Brewery in Durban – brews four beers mainly for their adjoining bar

Disappointing

- Castle Lager – nearly as bad as the best American beer

Beer must-do

- Visit the SAB World of Beer in Newtown, Johannesburg
- Follow the KwaZulu-Natal beer route

Other drinks

A word of warning on South Africa's other alcoholic beverages – BEWARE. Many of these moonshines could soon have you being fed by a tube at a nearby hospital, which in many instances would be an adventure in itself.

Witblits
A grappa made mainly in the Western Cape.

Mampoer

This bastard brother of witblits is made from any fruit other than grapes. It has fuelled legends and was the source for many of Herman Charles Bosman's tales of the Bushveld. It is firewater with an alcohol content often reaching a staggering 90 per cent proof.

Did you know?

In 1926 Herman Charles Bosman, hearing a disturbance in his stepbrother's bedroom in the Johannesburg suburb of Bellevue East, rushed in and shot him dead. He was sentenced to death, later commuted, and released on parole after nearly four years. His stories of prison are told in *Stone Cold Jug*.

Skokiaan

Do not even try this bootleg unless you want to become a zombie or corpse. Often spiked with methyl alcohol for extra kick, it has been featured in *Time* magazine as one of the world's deadliest drinks.

Did you know?

Skokiaan killed nine people and hospitalised 55 during a party in KwaZulu-Natal in 1956.

Lest you think we have a national death wish, along comes Amarula Cream, one of the most delectable liqueurs of its kind made from the fruit of the marula tree, which has long been the party staple for elephants and baboons.

Best bars

A good bar is a place that should capture the essential charm of the country, which we believe the following do:

- Khuwana Tavern in Mandela Village north of Pretoria – outrageously eccentric with mural art depicting orgies. Best fun anywhere
- The Church Bar in Pilgrim's Rest – once the chapel of a girl's school, it is still a spiritual place
- The Notties Pub in Nottingham Road – the oldest country establishment in KwaZulu-Natal, it is possessed by the ghost of a raunchy barkeeper who is reputed to still turn tricks
- Perseverance Tavern in Cape Town – the oldest bar in the country, it is little changed from when it was founded in 1808
- The Panty Bar in Paternoster – it is decorated with such appalling taste as to have an appeal all of its own. It takes its name from the panties hung from the ceiling of brides who are required to donate their underwear if they honeymoon here
- The Laird's Arms in Matjiesfontein – honky-tonk still resonates from this Victorian pub in the desert
- Die Mystic Boer in Bloemfontein – a middle finger to the staidness of Boer ancestry in the heart of Boer

ancestry
- The Star of the West in Kimberley – recaptures the wild days of the mining camp
- The Radium Beer Hall in Johannesburg – it well deserves its listing as one of the top 20 bars in the world
- Kwa-Thabeng in Soweto – encompasses the heart and soul of old Soweto jazz halls

Avoid

- Anything made of glass and brass
- Anything offering 'karaoke'

Best places for sundowners

- Llandudno Beach
- Robberg Nature Reserve
- Otter Trail, Storms River Mouth
- Camps Bay
- Golden Gate Highlands National Park
- Kings Walden, Agatha in Limpopo
- The Ambassador Hotel, Bantry Bay
- Drakensberg
- Skabenga's in Noordhoek
- Wilderness

SPORTS

Sports trivia

- The first rugby match in South Africa kicked off at Cape

Town's Green Point Common between a military and civilian side on 23 August 1862. The game had been introduced to the region at the city's Diocesan College (Bishops) the year before.

- The South African Rugby Board was constituted in 1889.
- English cricketers became the first to tour South Africa in 1889. Two of the matches were retrospectively given Test status, though the first official tour by England was only in 1905-1906.

Did you know?

The first international cricket game in South Africa was played, of all places, at Matjiesfontein in the Karoo in 1889.

- The first football association, the all-white Football Association of South Africa, was formed in 1892. Since then football has become the most popular sport in the country.
- Johannesburg cyclist Lourens Meintjies became South Africa's first ever world champion when he triumphed at the Chicago World's Fair in 1893.
- A South African rugby team toured Britain in 1906. On their return the members for the first time wore a golden springbok on the pocket of dark-green, gold-edged blazers. The Springbok would go on to become the insignia for most other sports until the first democratic elections in 1994, and appeared on army badges, South African Airways aircraft and railway coaches.
- Natal sprinter Reggie Walker became the first South African to take an Olympic gold medal when he won the 100 metres

in 10,8 seconds in 1908. He was not part of the national team, only making it to the games on funds raised by supporters.

- In 1921, 34 runners left Pietermaritzburg for Durban in what has become the annual Comrades Marathon, the world's ultimate ultra-marathon. The first race was to commemorate comrades who had fallen in World War I.

- Though the Springboks were considered one of the most powerful rugby forces in the world, they had never defeated the New Zealand All Blacks in an away tour. The New Zealanders were then considered the best international side, having never been beaten in a Test series on home soil, but the mantle passed to the South Africans when they won the third Test at Auckland's Eden Park 17-6 to take the series 2-1 on 25 September 1937.

- The last ever unlimited-time cricket Test match, known as the Timeless Test, began in Durban against England on 3 March 1939. It was abandoned after 12 days (nine of play) as the England side would have missed the boat home. It was also the longest Test match ever played.

- Eric Sturgess and Sheila Summers became South Africa's first Wimbledon tennis champions when they won the mixed doubles, beating John Bromwich and Louis Brough in 1949.

- Bobby Locke became the first South African golfer to win a major when he triumphed in the Open at Troon in Scotland in 1949.

Did you know?

South Africans have won more golf majors than players from any other country except America.

- Vic Toweel became South Africa's first boxing world champion when he defeated Manuel Ortiz to take the bantamweight title on 31 May 1950.
- Gert Potgieter set a world record for the 440 yards hurdles at the Commonwealth Games in Cardiff in 1958.
- Karen Muir, a 12-year-old Kimberley schoolgirl, broke the world 110-yard backstroke record in Blackpool, England in 1965.
- South African Gary Player became only the fifth golfer in history to win the Grand Slam (the game's four major championships – the US Masters, US Open, the Open and the US PGA) when he triumphed in the US Open in 1965. He would win another five 'majors', making him one of the sport's greats. Today he competes on the Senior Tour and designs golf courses, including those at Sun City.
- The Springbok cricket side beat England in a Test match at Trent Bridge by 94 runs inside four days on 9 August 1965. It marked the beginning of a five-year period in which South Africa dominated the sport, which ended when their political isolation began.
- September 1968 – Coloured Cape Town-born cricketer Basil D'Oliviera was included in an England side to tour South Africa. President BJ Vorster refused to accept the team, leading to the cancellation of the tour in September 1968. This gave impetus to anti-apartheid activists calling for a sports boycott of the country, which became near complete during the 1970s and 80s.
- South Africa was expelled from the International Olympic Committee in 1968.
- The South African team won the inaugural World Bowls Championships in 1972.

- The South African tennis team of Pat Pretorius, Brenda Kirk and Greta Delport won the Federation Cup in 1972.
- Surfer Shaun Tomson in 1977 became the only South African to win the IPS World Championship.
- Jody Scheckter, driving a Ferrari, became the first South African to win the world Formula 1 championship in 1979.
- Flyweight Peter 'The Terror' Mathebule became South Africa's first black boxing world champion when he beat Tae-Shik Kim at Los Angeles in 1980.
- Johan Kriek became the first South African to win a tennis major singles title when he won the Australian Open in January 1981. He would successfully defend his title the following year.

Did you know?

Four South African-born cricketers have captained England – Tony Greig, Allan Lamb, Kevin Pietersen and Andrew Strauss.

- With the series tied 1-1, the Springbok rugby team had the opportunity to again beat the All Blacks on home soil at Eden Park on 12 September 1981. The tour had been marked by anti-apartheid protests, but nothing on the scale of what took place in Auckland. As police battled demonstrators, the match was flour-bombed from a Cessna aircraft. On the field, the game was heading for a draw, but a debatable penalty in the dying moments won it for the hosts. This was the last tour during apartheid to a major rugby-playing nation.

- South African Zola Budd, running for Britain, made her home country and her quickly adopted one cringe when she tripped favourite Mary Decker in the 3 000-metre event.
- Wally Hayward became the first octogenarian to successfully complete the Comrades Marathon on 31 May 1989. A multiple winner of the event he first won in 1930, he once held time records for the 'up' and 'down' runs as well as for youngest and oldest victor. Despite Bruce Fordyce winning eight in a row (nine times overall) and setting numerous records, Hayward's is considered by some to be the greater achievement.
- The International Olympic Committee lifted the ban on South Africa in July 1991.
- On 24 June 1995 South Africa won the 3rd Rugby World Cup at its first attempt – having missed the previous two in 1987 and 1991 because of the sports boycott. The All Blacks were overwhelming favourites, but inspired by Mandela wearing the identical Number 6 jersey to captain Francois Pienaar, the Springboks won 15-12 in extra time when Joel Stransky kicked a drop goal from the sideline. The build-up to the final at Ellis Park in Johannesburg and the win contributed in no small measure to Mandela's tireless efforts at reconciliation.
- In 1996 the national football side, Bafana Bafana, coached by Clive Barker, won the African Nations Cup when they defeated Tunisia 2-0.
- South Africa participated in the Olympic Games in 1996 for the first time since 1960. Swimmer Penny Heyns won two gold medals and Josiah Thugwane triumphed with another gold in the men's marathon.
- Golfer Ernie Els became the first foreign player in 90 years in

1997 to win the US Open twice. This feat was repeated a few years later by Retief Goosen.

- South African cricket was thrown into turmoil when Proteas captain Hansie Cronje admitted to match fixing. Well, not quite: he claimed the devil made him do it.
- Baby Jake Matlala became the first South African to win four world titles when he defeated Colombian Juan Herrera for the WBU junior flyweight boxing championship in 2002.
- The International Cricket Council's eighth Cricket World Cup began in South Africa on 8 February 2003 with a glittering opening ceremony at Newlands cricket ground in Cape Town. The next day the Proteas (as the South African team became known) got off to a disastrous start by losing to the West Indies. It got worse and they did not make it beyond the pool stages.
- South Africa was thrown into a frenzy of celebration on 15 May 2004 as the announcement was made that the country would host the world's most popular sporting spectacle – the 2010 FIFA World Cup. The host cities are: Johannesburg, Pretoria, Cape Town, Bloemfontein, Nelspruit, Port Elizabeth, Polokwane and Durban.
- The Blue Bulls became the first South African franchise to win the Super 14 rugby title when they defeated the Sharks in Durban in 2007. They would triumph again in 2009.
- The Springboks became only the second team to win the Rugby World Cup twice, on 20 October 2007. Led by John Smit, they beat England 15-6 in the final at the Stade de France in Paris.
- South African golfer Trevor Immelman won the US Masters on 13 April 2008.
- Cricketers Neil McKenzie and Graeme Smith established a

new Test opening partnership of 415 against Bangladesh in March 2008.

- In December 2008 the Proteas became the first South African cricket team to win a Test series in Australia. They promptly lost the return series at home.
- The South African team won the rugby Sevens world title for the first time in 2009.
- In August 2009 Springbok rugby captain John Smith becomes the most capped skipper in the history of the game when he led the team for the 60th time.
- In September 2009 the Springboks were crowned Tri-Nations champions after victory over the All Blacks in Hamilton, New Zealand.

Best golf courses

- Leopard Creek, Malelane, Mpumalanga
- Links at Fancourt, George, Western Cape
- Gary Player Country Club at Sun City, North West
- Arabella Country Club, Kleinmond, Western Cape
- Durban Country Club, KwaZulu-Natal
- Pearl Valley, Winelands, Western Cape
- Fancourt Montagu, George, Western Cape
- Wild Coast Country Club, Port Edward, KwaZulu-Natal
- River Club, Johannesburg
- Royal J&K East, Johannesburg

Don't bother with . . .

- Hans Merensky is a great golf course; the problem is you have to go to Phalaborwa as part of the deal

Best places to pick up a hooker in South Africa *(for this we would like to acknowledge the in-depth research done by the Egyptian Confederation's Cup squad and Pakistani cricketers, though we are sorry to hear about their missing wallets)*

- Oxford Road in Johannesburg – but beware of male muggers dressed as women, as this could result in two surprises
- Mahatma Gandhi Road in Durban – all passion resistance goes out the window in what was once the notorious Point Road
- Voortrekker Road between Salt River and Belville in Cape Town – only a blowjob can make getting to Belville palatable. And we will resist every urge to play with the street name, which roughly translated means 'front puller'
- Any of the docklands of major ports – a gush of seamen
- William Nicol Drive round the Indaba Hotel in Fourways, Johannesburg – the climax of business at this award-winning conference centre

Avoid

- Hillbrow in Johannesburg – more dangerous than asphyxiation sex games

For more information on South Africa
go to www.southafrica.net

Index

Addo Elephant Park 123, 138
Adventure experiences, best 142
　　best airborne 144
　　best civilised 143
　　best water-based 143
African Resistance Movement 30
African Window 91
Afrikaans 23, 59
Afrikaner people 58-9
Agulhas National Park 124
Ai-Ais/Richtersveld National
　　Park 117
Airlines 74
ANC, founding 20
　　Youth League 24-5, 94
Ancestor worship 65
Andries-Ohrigstad 151
Anglo-Boer War, First 14, 104-5
Anglo-Boer War, Second 16, 17,
　　102, 105-7
Anglo-Zulu War, 1879 54, 102-4
Angolan War 32
Apartheid museum 99
Archaean period 5
Ardmore Ceramic Art 161
Area of SA 45
Arms Deal 41
Arts and crafts 161-2
　　best places to buy 162
Asian Culture 60

Augrabies Falls National Park
　　124

Bafana Bafana 191
Baker, Sir Herbert 84
Bambatha, Chief 19
Bantu Education 98
Barberspan 136
Barberton gold rush 153-4
Barnard, Chris 71
Bars, best 185
Battle of Blaauwberg 101
Battle of Muizenberg 101
Battlefields 101-7
Baxter Theatre 170
Beaches, best 141
　　Blue Flag 140-41
Beaufort Group 3
Beauty queen trivia 171
Beer 182-3
Bertha's Bill 23
Bertram House 83
Bhunga 87
Big Hole 86
Biggar, Alexander 10
Biko, Steve 32, 33, 88-9
　　Foundation 89
Biomes 119
Birdwatching 136-8
　　spots, top 138

Black Community Programme 32

Black Consciousness 32, 88

Black People's Convention 89

Blesbok Spruit 137

Blood River 12

Blue Bulls 192

Blyde River Canyon 118

Bo-Kaap Museum 83

Bontebok National Park 125

Boraine, Alex 36

Border Cave 6

Boschendal 178-9

Botanical Gardens 139

Botha, Jan Valentyn 151

Botha, Louis 19, 106

Botha, PW 32, 34

Bowls 189

Brand, Quintin 75

Bray, Edwin 153

Brenner, Sydney 71

Brewers, best 182

British occupation of Cape 101

Broederbond 22

Broom, Robert 90

Budd, Zola 191

Buitenverwachting 177

Burning Truth memorial 93

Bushmen 4, 53

Camdeboo National Park 125

Cape Floral Kingdom 113

Cape Minstrels 163

Cape West Coast biosphere 118

Cape winelands biosphere 118

Capital cities 19, 47

Capital punishment 76

Car, first 74, 75

Castle of Good Hope 7, 8, 83

Cato, GC 13

Cetshwayo 14, 102-3

Charlton Smith, Thomas 12, 13

Chelmsford, Lord 103

Christian National Education 18

Churches 65-6

Chweneyagae, Presley 168

Cinema, first 167

Cities, best places to chill 149

City vibe 149

Climate 45-6

Coat of arms 48

Codesa 37

Coelacanth 24

Coetzee, JM 173

Colley, George 104

Coloured people 59

Communications 72

Communist Party 22

Comrades Marathon 188, 191

Congella, Battle of 13

Congress of the People, Kliptown 27, 95

Congress Youth League 25

Constantia wine route 179

Constitution Hill 96

198   Cormack, Allan 71
Cradle of Humankind 111-12
Cricket trivia 187, 188, 189
Crime 76
Cronje, Hansie 192
Cultural villages 62-3
Cultural History Museum,
    National 91
Culture 159-94
Currency 70
Cycle routes, best 144

D'Oliviera, Basil 189
D'Urban, Sir Benjamin 10
da Gama, Vasco 114
Dakar Safari 36
Dance 166
Dart, Raymond 23
Dave Matthews Band 165
de Klerk, FW 36, 37, 86
De Hoop Vlei 136
de la Rey, Koos 16
de Melker, Daisy 77
De Mond State Forest 136
de Villiers, Abraham 178
de Villiers, Jean 178
de Wet, Quartus 30
Defence Force 20
Delport, Greta 190
Delville Wood 21, 90
Democratic elections, 1994 39,
    108
Demographics, *see* Population

Desert biome 122
Diamonds 68, 69, 87
Dias, Bartholomeu 4, 6, 7
Die Stem 27, 48-9
Dingane 9, 12
Dinosaurs 3,5
District Six 31, 84
    Museum 84
Drakensberg Boys Choir School
    115
Drakensberg Mountains 115
Drinks, local alcoholic 183-5
Drives, best 76
Dube, Rev John 20
Durban, origins 11
Dutch East India Company 7,
    83, 175

Economic trivia 68
Economy 67
Elephant Coast 116
Els, Ernie 192
Emblems, national 48
English culture 60
Eufees Trek 24
Eureka city 154
Excelsior Affair 41
Ezemvelo KZN parks 123-33

Farewell, George 10
Festivals, best 171
Film 167-8
First, Ruth 27

Fishing spots, best 145-6
Flag 23, 47, 48
Flight, first 74
Food, traditional 173-5
Football trivia 187
Fordyce, Bruce 191
Forest biome 121
Fort Frederick 9
Fossil sites 111
Franschhoek Oesfees 180
Franschhoek wine route 180
Freedom Charter 27, 85, 95
Freedom Park 100
Freedom Struggle, *see* Struggle
  for Freedom
Frelimo 32
French Huguenots 8, 176, 178
Frontier Wars, Eastern Cape 102
Fynbos biome 119
Fynn, Henry Francis 10, 11

Gallo, Eric 164
Gandhi, Mohandas (Mahatma)
  15, 93-4, 96, 105
  Memorial, Burning truth 93
Garden Route National Park
  125
Gemsbok National Park 126
Ghost towns 151-6
  Eastern Escarpment 152-6
  Great Trek 151-6
Gold, early prospectors 152-6

Eastern Escarpment discovery   199
  151
  Witwatersrand discovery 69
Golden Gate Highlands
  National Park 126
Golf courses, best 193
Gondolin 111
Gondwana 3, 5
Goosen, Retief 192
Gordimer, Nadine 173
Gordon Highlanders 104
Government 46
Grahamstown, founding 9
  Arts Festival 9, 60
Grasslands biome 119-20
Great Trek 11, 17
  ghost towns 151-6
Great Zimbabwe 6, 62
Greater Mapungubwe
  Transfrontier Park 126
Greenstone Belt 3, 5
Greig, Tony 190
Groot Constantia 83, 176-7
Group Areas Act 26, 99
Gumboot dance 57
Gwangwa, Jonas 164

Hani, Chris 38
Harris, Frederick 30
Hayward, Wally 191
Health 70-71
Hector Peterson Museum 98-9
Helderberg 75

Heritage sites 101-8
Hertzog, Albert 24
Heyns, Penny 191
Hiking trails, best 145
Historic attractions 79-108
Historic timeline 5-41
Hlobane 14
Hluhluwe-Imfolozi Game
    Reserve 131
Hoare, Mike 34
Homelands 28, 30
Hood, Gavin 168
Hookers 194
Huddleston, Trevor 26, 27
Huguenots 8, 176, 178

Ibrahim, Abdullah 164
Idasa 36
Immelman, Trevor 192
Immigrant culture 61-2
Immorality Act 26
Indian resistance campaign 93-4
Info Scandal 34, 41
Intombi Spruit 14
Iron Age 6, 112
Isandlwana 14, 102, 103, 104
iSimangaliso Wetland Park 116
Islam 67
Ithala Game Reserve 132

Jameson, Leander Starr 16
Jameson Raid 16, 41
Jamestown 154-5

Jennings, Alfred 72
Joseph, Helen 27
Judaic culture 61-2

Kalahari Gemsbok National
    Park 126
Kani, John 170
Karoo National Park 126
Kathrada, Ahmed 30, 97
Kgalagadi Transfrontier Park
    126, 138
uKhahlamba Drakensberg
    World Heritage Site 115
Khoi 4, 6
Khoikhoi 107
Khoikhoi-Dutch Wars 101
Khosi Bay System 137
Kimberley Mine Museum 86
King Kong 164
King, Dick 11, 13
King, James 10
Kirk, Brenda 190
Kirstenbosch National
    Botanical Garden 113
Kitchener, Lord 106
Klein Constantia 177
Kliptown 94
Klug, Aaron 70
Knysna National Lake Area 125
Kogelberg biosphere 118
Koopmans-De Wet House 83
Kramats 67
Kriek, Johan 190

Kromdraai 23, 111
Kruger National Park 127-8
Kruger to canyons biosphere 118
Kruger, Paul 15, 17
Kwaito 164
Kwela 163

Ladysmith Black Mambazo 165
Lake Sibaya 137
Lamb, Allan 190
Landform 45
Langebaan 6, 130, 136, 138
Langenhoven, CJ 27, 49
le Long, Jean 178
Lemba tribe 62
Lembede, Anton 25
Leyds, WJ 155
Leydsdorp 155-6
Liliesleaf Farm 30, 97-8
Linda, Solomon 164
Literature 172-3
Little Foot 111
Location of SA 45
Locke, Bobby 188
Lower Tugela 103
Luthuli, Albert 29, 85
Lydenburg 151

Mabasa, Noria 86
Machel, Samora 32
Majuba Hill 14, 102, 104
Makana 10

Makeba, Miriam 164, 165
Malan, DF 21, 23
Mammals 133-4
Manaka, Matsemela 170
Mandela, Nelson 22, 25, 27, 30, 37, 38, 39-40, 86, 87-8, 96, 97, 107, 108, 114
    Museum 87
Manim, Manny 169
Maponya, Maishe 170
Mapungubwe 6, 62, 112
    Museum 113
    Transfrontier Park 126
Marabi 163
Marakele National Park 128
Marievale Bird Sanctuary 138
Maritz, Gerrit 12
Market Theatre 169
Masakela, Hugh 164
Mashiyane, Spokes 163
Mass murders 77
Mathebule, Peter 'The Terror' 190
Matlala, Baby Jake 192
Matshikiza, Todd 164
Matthews, ZK 95
Mbaqanga 163
Mbeki, Govan 30, 97
Mbeki, Thabo 40
Mbulu, Letta 164
McKenzie, Neil 193
McLachlan, Tom 153
Mda, Peter 25

Mda, Zakes 170
Media 166-9
Medical trivia 71
Meintjies, Lourens 187
Mfecane 8
Mhlaba, Raymond 97
Military History, South African National Museum of 90
Milner, Lord Alfred 18
Miracle Cave, *see* Wonderwerk Cave
MK, *see* Umkhonto we Sizwe
Mkhuze Game Reserve 132, 138
Modjadji Cycad Reserve 139
Moerdijk, Gerhard 92
Mofolo Art centre 161
Mokala National Park 128
Monkeybiz ceramics 161
Monomotapa 153
Monuments, *see* Museums and monuments
Moshoeshoe, King 55
Mosques 67
Mothopeng, Zeph 28
Motlanthe, Kgalema 40
Mountain Zebra National Park 128
Msomi, Welcome 170
Muir, Karen 189
Mulder, Connie 34
Murchison Range 155
Murders, unsolved 78
Museum Afrika 92

Museums and monuments 81-101
    Eastern Cape 87-9
    Gauteng 89-100
    Northern Cape 86-7
    Western Cape 82-6
Music 163-6
Mvezo 87

Nama Karoo biome 122
Namaqua National Park 129
Namaqualand 121-2, 129
Napier, Sir George 12
Natal, early history 12, 13, 15
Natal Indian Congress 93
National anthem 16, 48-9, 50
National Cultural History Museum 91
National parks 123-33
National Party 20, 21, 22, 23, 99
    victory, 1948 25
Native Land Act 21
Natural attractions 109-46
Natural History, Transvaal Museum of 89
Ndebele people 56
Ndlovu, Hastings 33, 99
Ndumo Reserve 137, 138
Ndwandwe-Zulu War 102
Nelson Mandela Museum 87
Newspaper industry, early 69
Nkosi Sikelel' iAfrika, history 16
Nobel Peace Prize 29, 36, 38, 85

Nobel Square 85
Nongqawuse 14
Northern Flagship Institution 89
Nuclear weapons 38
NUSAS 88
Nxumalo, Gideon 164
Nylsvley 138

Official languages 52
Old Fort, Constitution Hill 96
Orange Free State, Boer Republic 13
Orange River Mouth Wetland 136
Ossewabrandwag 31
Outdoor activities and adventures 142-6

Paarl wine route 179-80
Pan Africanist Congress (PAC) 28, 95
Parks 122-33
    best of 130
Paton, Alan 172
Patterson, 'Wheelbarrow' Alex 153
Peace of Vereeniging 17
Perold, Abraham 176
Peterson, Hector 33, 98-9
    Museum 98-9
Photogenic hot spots 132
Pienaar, Francois 191

Pietermaritzburg, origins 12
Pietersen, Kevin 190
Pilgrim's Rest 153
Pityana, Barney 32
Plaatje, Sol 20, 172
Planetarium 82
Player, Gary 189
Ples, Mrs 23, 90, 111
Polokwane 40
Population 52-62
Population Registration Act 26, 99
uPoqo 30
Port Elizabeth 9
Port Natal 10
Post Office Tree 72, 82
Postberg Flower Reserve 130
Potchefstroom, origins 151
Potgieter, Andries 151
Potgieter, Gert 189
Pretoria, early history 14
Pretorius, Andries 12
Pretorius, Marthinus Wessels 14
Pretorius, Pat 190
Progressive Party 28
Prohibition of Mixed Marriages Act 26
Promotion of Bantu Self-Government Act 27
Proteas 193
Provinces 47
Public holidays 51
Pubs 185

204   Pulleine, Henry 103

Qunu 87

Radio, first broadcast 167
Rail disasters 73-4
Rainfall 46
Ramsar Sites 136-7
Rand Revolt 22
Rathebe, Dolly 164
Red Location Museum 87
Red Route 180
Referendum, 1960 29
    1983 35
Religion 63-6
Republic of SA 29
Retief, Piet 12
Rhodes, Cecil John 15, 16, 69, 84
Rhodes Memorial 84
Richtersveld 117, 122
Riotous Assemblies Act 27
Rivonia Treason Trial 30
Robben Island 85, 114
Robert, Auguste 'French Bob' 153, 155
Roberts, Lord 17, 106
Rock art 119
Rorke's Drift 102, 103, 104
Royal visit, 1947 25
Rugby trivia 186-7, 188
Rust en Vreugt 83

SAA 74
SABC 167
SABRA 26
San 53, 90
Sanctuaries, top 134-5
Sangomas 65
Savannah biome 121
Savimbi, Jonas 32
Scandals, best political 41
Scheckter, Jody 190
Schoeman, Stephanus 152
Schoemansdal 152
Schreiner, Olive 172
Schreuders, Claudette 86
Seasons 46
Seejarim, Usha 93
Seekoeivlei 137
Segregation, early 18
Selati Gold Fields 155
Selati Railway Company 155
Seme, Pixley 20
Semenya, Caiphas 164
Separate Representation of Voters Act 27
Serial killers 77
Seth, Abdulla 15
Settlers, 1820 10
Settlers Monument, 1820 60
Seychelles coup, 1981 34-5
Shaka 8-9, 10, 54, 57, 102, 116
Shangaan-Tsonga people 57
Sharpeville Human Rights Precinct 95

Sharpeville Massacre 29, 95, 107
Sheba Reef 154
Shipwrecks 73, 124
Shuttleworth, Mark 70
iSimangaliso Wetland Park 116
Simon, Barney 169
Simon's Town 8
Sisulu, Walter 25, 97
Skilpad Wildflower Reserve 129
Slabbert, Frederick van Zyl 36
Slave Lodge 83
Slavery 11
Small towns 150-58
    best of 156-7
Smith, Graeme 193
Smith, John 193
Smuts, Jan 22, 24
Sobukwe, Robert 28, 85, 95
Solomons, Bertha 23
Somerset, Lord Charles 9, 10
Sontonga, Enoch 16, 49-50
Sophiatown 26, 66, 163
Soshangane 57
Sotho people 55
South African Atomic Energy
    Board 70
South African Bureau for Racial
    Affairs 99
South African Museum and
    Planetarium 82
South African National
    Convention 19
South African National

Museum of Military History   205
    90
South African National Party 20
South African Native
    Convention 19
South African Native National
    Congress 20
South African Party 20
South African Railways and
    Harbours 75, 167
South African Students'
    Organisation 32, 88
South West Africa, occupation
    21
Southern apemen 3, 4, 5
Soweto Gospel Choir 165
Soweto, early beginnings 18
Soweto Uprising, 1976 33, 89,
    99
Space Theatre 170
Spitskop 153
Sports 186-94
    see also Outdoor activities and
    adventures 142-6
Springboks 192
Springbokvlakte 122
Stamps, first 72
State of emergency, 1960 95
    1985 36
Stellenbosch wine route 179
Sterkfontein Caves 23, 111
Sterkfontein Valley 3, 111
Steve Biko Foundation 89

Steve Biko Memorial 88
Steynsdorp 154-5
Stransky, Joel 191
Strauss, Andrew 190
Strijdom, JG 26
Struggle for Freedom 92, 93, 99,
    107-8
  best sites 100
Succulent Karoo biome 121-2
Sundowners, best places for 186
Surfing spots, best 146
Suzman, Helen 28
Swartkrans 112
Swazi people 56
Symbols, national 47

Taal Monument 59
Table Mountain National Park
    113
Tambo, Oliver 25, 32
Tankwa Karoo National Park
    129
Taung Child 22
Television 166-7
  infamous moments 168-9
Theatre 169-71
  history 169
Theatres, best 171
Theiler, Max 71
Theron, Charlize 167
Thugwane, Josiah 191
Thulamela 6, 62
Tolkien, JRR 115, 172

Tomlinson Commission 27
Tomson, Shaun 190
Tongaland 137
Touws River Gorge 125
Toweel, Vic 189
Trafford, William 153
Trains 73
Transfrontier parks 123-33
Transportation 72-5
Transvaal Museum of Natural
    History 89
Transvaal Museum, see National
    Cultural History Museum
Transvaal Republic 13
Truth and Reconciliation
    Commission 40
Tsafendas, Dimitrio 31
Tsitsikamma 6
Tsitsikamma National Park 125
Tsonga, see Shangaan-Tsonga
Tsotsi 168
Tswana people 56
Thukela Falls 116
Tutu, Desmond 36, 40, 85

uKhahlamba Drakensberg
    World Heritage Site 115
Ulundi, Battle of 103
Umkhonto we Sizwe 30, 88, 97,
    108
UNESCO Biosphere Reserves
    117-19
Union of South Africa 19

UNITA 32
United Party 20, 23
uPoqo 30
Utrecht 103
Uys, Jamie 167
Uys, Piet 12

van Coehoorn, Menno 7
van der stel, Simon 176-7
van der Stel, Willem 41, 177
van Deventer, Jaap 17, 107
van Riebeeck, Jan 7, 83, 175
van Ryneveld, Pierre 75
Venda people 57-8
Vergelegen 177-8
Verloren Vallei Nature Reserve 137
Verlorenvlei 136
Verwoerd, Hendrik 17, 27, 29, 31
Vhembe biosphere 119
Vilakaze Street 39
Voëlvry tour 165
von Wouw, Anton 93
Voortrekker Monument 92
Voortrekkers 151
Vorster, BJ 31
Vredefort Dome 3, 5, 112

Walker, Reggie 187
Wakkerstroom 137
War Museum 90

War of Independence 14, 104
Water-based adventures, best 143
Waterberg biosphere 119
Watson, Lyall 172
West Coast National Park 130
Weston, John 74
Wetlands 116, 136-7
Wilderness Lakes 136
Wilderness National Park 125
William Fehr Collection 83
Wine 175-82
Wine estates, best 181
    historic 176-9
Wine routes 179-80
    Constantia 179
    Franschhoek 180
    Paarl 179-80
    Stellenbosch 179
    Worcester 180
Women's Enfranchisement Bill 23
Women's Prison, Constitution Hill 96
Wonderwerk Cave 5
Worcester wine route 180
World Cup, 2010 FIFA 192
World Heritage Sites 111-17
World War I 21
Woza Albert! 170

Xhosa people 54-5

208 Zoos 158

Zoutpansberg Maatschappij 152

Zoutpansbergdorp 152

Zulu people 54

Zululand 102-3, 116, 131

  Birding Route 138

  early history 14-15

Zuma, Jacob 40, 41